Leader to Leader

NUMBER 40   SPRING 2006

Hesselbein + Company

Executive Forum

From the Front Lines

From the Editors

Peter Drucker

His inspiration and wisdom will be with us forever.

Peter Drucker, the inspiration for the Peter F. Drucker Foundation for Nonprofit Management and its honorary chairman from its founding in 1991 until 2002, when it was succeeded by the Leader to Leader Institute, passed away on November 11, 2005. It was just a few days before our Winter issue was due at the printer, and we could do little to acknowledge our loss besides including his picture inside our front cover. With this Spring issue, we do want to acknowledge Peter's life and work and commemorate his passing.

Peter Drucker had long been hailed in the United States and abroad as the seminal thinker, writer, and lecturer on the contemporary organization. In 1997, he was featured on the cover of *Forbes* magazine under the headline, "Still the Youngest Mind," and *Business Week* has called him "the most enduring management thinker of our time."

It was a sad day when we said good-bye to Peter, yet his inspiration and wisdom will be with us forever. Peter's belief that all institutions in society must look out for the common good and together strive toward a functioning society will always resonate in the work of the Leader to Leader Institute.

At his passing, the press readily acknowledged his unique contribution. "He was justly lauded and adored as the greatest management thinker and writer of all time," *Fortune* said. "Smart ideas, clever insight, and pragmatic philosophy distinguish Drucker as the most enduring and influential management guru in history," *Business Week* wrote in a major cover story. The *Wall Street Journal* called Peter simply "an American sage," adding that he was "the most influential management thinker of the past century." The *Washington Post* noted, "his work influenced Winston Churchill, Bill Gates, Jack Welch, and the Japanese business establishment," citing only a famous few out of millions.

The *New York Times* highlighted Peter's "view that big business and nonprofit enterprises were the defining innovation of the 20th century," which, the *Times* said, "led him to pioneering social and management theories." And *USA Today* rightly observed that Peter's work extended far beyond management, calling him "one of the most important social theorists of the past century."

Perhaps this last observation was what was most heartening to us at *Leader to Leader.* For Peter's work was about much more than efficiency, profits, or even innovation. As Peter's friend and colleague Joseph Maciariello wrote in our Summer 2005 issue, "If you read his 65 years of work, you will see a man devoted to liberty, to institutions that function, to management, to individual achievement, to individual social status and function, to community, and to values that we in free societies widely share." While much of the business press seemed to ignore Peter's larger contributions to our society, others did not. The *USA Today* article quoted earlier continues, "Good management, he believed, was not principally about improving third-quarter profits but about building a better world. Societies with well-run public and private institutions would be healthier, wealthier, and more just. . . . His modest brilliance seems a bit quaint in today's world of the self-aggrandizing, multimillionaire CEO. Perhaps that's all the more reason he needs to be rediscovered." And the *New York Times* noted as well, "While Drucker loved dazzling audiences with his wit and wisdom, his goal was not to be known as an oracle. Instead, his views about where the world was headed generally arose out of advocacy for what he saw as moral action."

Peter's advocacy for moral action was always very real. In the end, we remember Peter mostly for what he was to us at the Leader to Leader Institute, a supportive adviser and a warm and kind friend.

Leader to Leader

Frances Hesselbein
Editor-in-Chief

Alan Shrader
Managing Editor

Keith Timko
Senior Editor

Peter Economy
Associate Editor

Jo-Ann Wasserman
Editorial Director

Alice Rowan
Production Editor

Frank Welsch
Production Manager

Elizabeth Phillips
Editorial Assistant

Hilary Powers
Copy Editor

Yvo Riezebos
Creative Director

Images.com/CORBIS
Cover image

Sackett Design Associates
Design

Leigh McLellan Design
Composition and Technical Art

Leader to Leader Institute

■

*"To strengthen
the leadership of the
social sector"*

■

Leader to Leader (print ISSN 1087-8149, on-line ISSN 1531-5355 at Bold Ideas, www.bold-ideas.com) is published quarterly by the Leader to Leader Institute and Wiley Subscription Services, Inc., A Wiley Company, at Jossey-Bass, 989 Market St., San Francisco, CA 94103-1741. Copyright © 2006 by the Leader to Leader Institute. All rights reserved. **Jossey-Bass:** Debra S. Hunter, President; Susan Lewis, Vice President and Publisher, Periodicals; Cedric Crocker, Vice President, Business and Management; Paul Foster, Vice President, Education, Religion, Health, Psychology; James Thomson, Vice President, Marketing and Sales; Susan Call, Vice President, Human Resources; Michael Goldstein, Circulation Manager; Julianne Ososke, Senior Manufacturing Supervisor; Joe Schuman, Subscriptions Manager. **Permission to copy:** No part of this issue may be reproduced in any form without permission in writing from the Leader to Leader Institute and Jossey-Bass. For inquiries, write Permissions Dept., c/o John Wiley & Sons, Inc., 111 River Street, Hoboken, NJ 07030. Periodicals postage paid at San Francisco, CA, and additional mailing offices. **Postmaster:** Send address changes to *Leader to Leader,* Jossey-Bass, 989 Market St., San Francisco, CA 94103-1741. Manufactured in the United States of America on acid-free recycled paper containing at least 20 percent postconsumer waste. **Subscriptions:** $250 institutional, $199 individuals, $99 U.S. 501(c)(3) nonprofit organizations; additional postage charges apply to subscribers outside the U.S. **To order: call toll-free (888) 378-2537, fax toll-free (888) 481-2665, write Jossey-Bass, 989 Market Street, San Francisco, CA 94103-1741, or e-mail jbsubs@jbp.com. Outside the United States, call (415) 433-1740 or fax (415) 951-8553. For article reprints of 100 copies or more, please call Craig Woods at (201) 748-8771 or e-mail cwoods@wiley.com.**

Peter Drucker's Light Shines On

Frances Hesselbein

This is the column I hoped never to have to write—the column that would mark the moment we said goodbye to Peter Drucker.

We have lost the quiet, powerful intellect, the warm and generous friend. Peter redefined the social sector, redefined society, redefined leadership and management—and gave mission, innovation, and values powerful new meanings that have changed our lives.

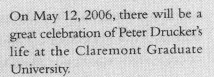

I've had the privilege of sitting at the feet of Peter Drucker since 1981, participating in the founding of the Peter Drucker Foundation for Nonprofit Management, being one of those fortunate few who, in 1990 and for the next 12 years, could listen and learn from him as he attended Drucker Foundation board meetings and conferences, participated in our video conferences, and advised in the development of our tools and books and videotapes. His philosophy permeated every aspect of our Drucker Foundation/Leader to Leader Institute initiatives, and will continue to do so.

When I learned of Peter's death, I was speaking at a conference in Tampa, so I returned to New York and flew to California in time to attend the small, private memorial service at St. John's Episcopal Church on Monday afternoon, November 14, in LaVerne.

Doris Drucker, their four children and six grandchildren, Bob and Linda Buford, John Bachmann, Claremont Graduate University representatives, old friends, and I were part of the small group of 25 who gathered to celebrate his life. The Druckers' son Vincent, their daughter Cecily, and John Bachmann spoke; there was the liturgy, and the service ended with a quiet, moving singing of "Amazing Grace."

On May 12, 2006, there will be a great celebration of Peter Drucker's life at the Claremont Graduate University.

I remember when I took my first professional position as executive director of Talus Rock Girl Scout Council in Johnstown, Pennsylvania, long ago in 1970. As I walked into the office that first morning I had under my arm a copy of Peter Drucker's *The Effective Executive* for each member of the staff. I had no idea who he was. I just knew his book was exactly right for our work. Six years later when I was called to New York to become the national executive director, CEO of the Girl Scouts of the USA, *The Effective Executive* traveled to New York with me, as did every book Peter had ever published.

Perhaps if I share with you how I met Peter and the influence he has had upon my work, it may be one more story to add to the thousands of how Peter influenced, encouraged, and challenged leaders to be leaders. All of us treasure his wisdom so generously shared.

I met Peter in 1981 when as CEO of the Girl Scouts of the USA I was invited by the chancellor of New York University to join 50 foundation and other social sector presidents for dinner, to hear the great Peter Drucker speak. I knew that in

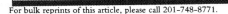

such a large group I would not have an opportunity to meet him, but I would have the opportunity to hear him live—Peter Drucker, the great thought leader who had influenced the volunteers and staff in the largest organization for girls and women in the world.

The invitation was for a 5:30 P.M. reception at the University Club in New York to be followed by dinner and Professor Drucker's address. Now, if you grow up in the mountains of western Pennsylvania, 5:30 is 5:30, so I arrived promptly at the University Club, only to find myself at the reception alone with two bartenders.

I turned, and behind me was a man. Obviously, if one grows up in Vienna, 5:30 is 5:30. The man said, "I am Peter Drucker."

Startled, I responded with, "Do you know how important you are to the Girl Scouts?" He said, "No, tell me."

"If you go to any one of our 335 Girl Scout Councils, you will find a shelf of your books. If you read our corporate planning monograph, and study our management and structure, you will find your philosophy," I replied.

Peter said, "You are very daring. I would be afraid to do that. Tell me, does it work?"

"It works superbly well," I replied. "And I have been trying to gather up enough courage to call you and ask if I may have an hour of your time, if I may come to Claremont and lay out before you everything you say the effective organization must have in place. We do. And I'd like to talk with you about how we take the lead in this society and blast into the future."

Peter replied, "Why should both of us travel? I'll be in New York in several months and I'll give you a day of my time." And that was the beginning of eight years of the remarkable adventure in learning and exploration the Girl Scouts were privileged to have with the father of modern management.

The great day came in the spring of 1981 when Peter Drucker met with members of the Girl Scout National Board and staff for the first time. Thus began a remarkable journey for us as he helped us answer those Five Drucker questions:

What is our mission?

Who is our customer?

What does the customer value?

What have been our results?

What is our plan?

I can hear his voice: "If you don't end up with a plan, a good time was had by all, and that is all." The auditorium

of the Girl Scout Edith Macy Conference Center at Briarcliff Manor, Westchester County, New York, is named for Peter Drucker.

When I left the Girl Scouts of the USA, January 31, 1990, I bought a home in Easton, Pennsylvania, promised a publisher I would write a book on mission, and wasn't going to travel so much. But in mid-March, six weeks later, Bob Buford, Dick Schubert, and I (all of us enormously influenced by Peter in our careers) flew to Claremont to brainstorm a way to permeate the nonprofit sector with Peter's works, his philosophy. The day before Peter was to join us, we brainstormed all afternoon and evening and the result was the Peter Drucker Foundation for Nonprofit Management, a foundation that would deal not in money but in intellectual capital, and that would move the Drucker philosophy across the nonprofit world.

The next morning Peter arrived to meet us not knowing what we were up to. Newsprint covered the walls of our meeting room, and we took turns presenting our wonderful brainchild. Peter listened with no expression; we couldn't tell what he was thinking. Finally, "We will not name it for me. I am not dead yet and I do not intend to be an icon." (He lost that battle.) "We will not focus on me; there are a lot of good people out there and you will bring them in." (Already he had expanded our vision.)

Bob said that he and Dick thought I should be the chairman of the board. After all, I had just left the Girl Scout position and would have time to chair several board meetings a year for the new Drucker Foundation. Peter's response: "You will not be the Chairman, you will be the president and CEO and run it or it won't work." So six weeks after leaving one of the largest voluntary organizations in the world, I found myself the CEO of the smallest foundation in the world, with no staff and no money, just a powerful vision shared with co-founders passionate about bringing Peter to the wider world, transforming a sector that soon Peter Drucker would name "the social sector" because he believed it is in this sector that we find the greatest success in meeting social needs. The rest is history, well documented and alive on our Web site (www.leadertoleader.org), in our 20 books in 28 languages traveling around the world, and in this journal.

It is difficult to think about Peter without remembering his gracious manners, the power of civility that was so much a part of who he was and how he did what he did, a "gift of example." He was enormously generous with his time and his counsel. After that first transforming day with the Girl Scouts, he gave us several days of his time for the next eight years, just as he would pour his time, energy, and wisdom into the Drucker Foundation for the next twelve years. We learned about passion for the vision, the mission, from Peter, and thousands of our members, authors, and participants shared it with a new kind of exuberance as we documented his impact, his influence.

There are many of us who walk around remembering and trying to live up to his expectations of us: "Think first. Speak last." We remember how at Drucker Foundation Board meetings he would sit quietly, listening to every word, and then at that magic moment respond with the Drucker insight, and in a few powerful sentences clarify the issue, broaden the vision, move us into the future. Honoring the past but intensely defining the future was one of his great gifts.

For example, he wrote that we would see the reunification of Germany when no one else was making that statement. When the day came and the reunification was taking place, he was asked how he could have predicted this. His reply: "I never predict. I simply look out the window and see what is visible but not yet seen." In our tenuous times, when few attempt to "pre-dict" the future, that one statement of Peter's philosophy encourages and inspires those who would be leaders of the future to "look out the window" as Peter did and "see what is visible but not yet seen."

Each of us has our own stories; all of us are better for having our moments with this quiet, courteous giant who for a while walked among us, with more questions than answers, thinking first, speaking last, as he counseled us to do. From 1990 on, over the next twelve years, as the Drucker Foundation and then as the Leader to Leader Institute, there are hundreds of moments and messages we captured and treasure; yet for this column I should like to focus on his work and his messages about the nonprofit, the social sector, for he did redefine, bring new recognition, new significance to the social sector as the equal partner of business and government. We hear his voice: "It is not business, it is not government, it is the social sector that may yet save the society."

Some of us may remember his seminal article in the July-August 1989 *Harvard Business Review*, "What Business Can Learn from Nonprofits." (Some were sure it had to be a typo before they read the article, which turned on its head the old view of the nonprofit sector as somehow the junior partner of business and government.) But

Peter said, "The best-managed nonprofit is better managed than the best-managed corporation."

Peter forced this voluntary sector "to see itself life-size," and he changed the face of the social sector. When Peter came to that first meeting with the Girl Scout National Board and management team, he told us, after thanking us for permitting him to be there, "You do not see yourselves life-size. You do not appreciate the significance of your work, for we live in a society that pretends to care about its children, and it does not." And then he added, "For a little while you give a girl an opportunity to be a girl in a society that forces her to grow up all too soon."

Three years ago I was writing about children at risk and I called Peter and asked, "In 1981 you said, 'We live in a society that pretends to care about its children and it does not.' Do you still feel the same way?" Silence, then, "Frances, has anything changed?" Always Peter distilled the language until the message connected. Short, powerful, compelling. We never forget his words, and his message about our children grows in intensity.

He lived to see the vast proliferation of college and university nonprofit management programs, centers for social enterprise—hundreds across the country and the world. And we can hear his voice, "Management is a liberal art." One last area of massive influence, of the many we could list, is his achievement in bringing business leaders to see the community as the responsibility of the corporation: "Leaders in every single institution and in every single sector ... have *two responsibilities*. They are responsible and accountable for the performance of their institutions, and that requires them and their institutions to be concentrated, focused, limited. They are responsible also, however, for the community as a whole."

One measurable result of how Peter inspired leaders across the sectors to collaborate for the greater good is that collaboration, alliances, and partnerships across the three sectors, building the healthy community that cares about all of its people, became the powerful shared vision of principled corporate leadership and their social sector partners.

On our 15th Anniversary, April 2005, we celebrated Peter Drucker's life and contribution at our "Shine a Light" dinner. "Shine a Light" was appropriate that evening, and is now, for that's what Peter did for 95 years. His light illuminates the darkness, inspiring young people just discovering Peter, our young leaders of the future who are finding relevance and inspiration just as our leaders of the present have found this Drucker philosophy the indispensable companion for their journey. For the Leader to Leader Institute it is not enough to "keep his legacy alive." Instead, we will bring new energy, new resources, new partnerships to our new challenge. Peter's light shines across the sectors, reaching leaders hungry for Peter's messages that will illuminate, will change their lives, and in the end will move them to define the effective executive, the leader of the future. That will be the living legacy of Peter Drucker: vibrant, alive for a new generation, with new relevance, new challenge, new significance, new celebration of Peter Drucker's life, his influence, his light that shines anew.

Frances Hesselbein is editor-in-chief of Leader to Leader, founding president of the Drucker Foundation, chairman of the board of governors of the Leader to Leader Institute, and former chief executive of the Girl Scouts of the U.S.A. Her most recent book is "Hesselbein on Leadership."

Ten Rules for Leaders

Charles F. Knight

In 1973, when I became CEO of Emerson, I was thirty-seven years old and had a tough act to follow. My predecessor, W. R. "Buck" Persons, had led the company for 19 years and initiated its continuing transformation from a medium-sized producer of electric motors and fans with a defense contracting business into a strong, diversified manufacturing corporation. The Persons era was a time of great prosperity for the company, its employees, and its stockholders.

During the next 27 years, with the help of many thousands of energetic, committed employees, we instituted and refined the Emerson management process, and it delivered. Between 1973 and 2000, when I stepped down as CEO, the company's sales rose more than fifteen-fold, to more than $15 billion in fiscal 2000, and net earnings increased eighteen-fold, to more than $1.4 billion.

Emerson's record of increased earnings per share and dividends each year for these 27 consecutive years is among the longest for consistent performance in American business.

A critical element of the management process is leadership, which we define as creating an environment in which people can and do make a difference. Leadership is a subjective matter, and there is no single correct view of what makes a good leader. My own view of what works best in an organization is presented here.

I like to make lists and especially lists of ten points. Many times I'll write a long list of points about a topic and stew over it for a while, then do some sorting and arranging, trying to understand the relationships. If possible, I'll boil the list down to ten points. Cutting the list shorter risks blurring distinctions and burying key points; making it longer is undisciplined. Ten is not a magic number, but getting the points right stretches the mind.

Following are my ten attributes of effective leaders, the ten keys to creating an environment in which people can and do make a difference. As individual points, they may seem obvious. Collectively and cumulatively, however, they help create the environment for exceptional organizational performance.

1. Be Committed to Success

Leadership starts here, with a commitment to success. We all see people we know will succeed, and most of them pour enormous energy into projects or assignments. They also have the perseverance to stay with an issue or a problem until it gets resolved. That combination of energy and perseverance is central to the commitment to success. And that commitment is contagious. It galvanizes an organization, big or small. And obviously, people like to be on a winning team. Similarly, people quickly spot a lack of commitment. That too is contagious, and it drags down performance.

2. Set Proper Priorities

No one disagrees with the critical importance of setting proper priorities, but time after time, I've seen

 Adapted with permission of Harvard Business School Press from *Performance Without Compromise: How Emerson Consistently Achieves Winning Results* by Charles F. Knight.

organizations struggle because their leaders didn't or couldn't do it.

They typically get in trouble for three reasons. First, it takes hard work and hard thinking to identify a limited number of actions and communicate them in a clear, logical sequence—to keep things simple. Second, leaders may pursue the wrong priorities, but they are just as likely—maybe more likely—to be unsure of what the right priorities should be, especially in a fast-changing world. They don't take the time and do the work to get their priorities right. Third, leaders often experience difficulty in managing the trade-off among conflicting objectives, such as profit and growth. They don't know which to attack, in which order, and how moving in one direction affects progress in another.

The need to set the right priorities is one reason Emerson invests so much time in planning and re-planning. Some people think we're nuts because we replan every business every year. However, our planning process and cycle gives us repeated opportunities to examine and question our assumptions and identify what's important. Planning also gives us the discipline to keep asking questions and to keep resetting priorities when circumstances change.

An important aspect of setting priorities is to communicate them to the people who must understand them and follow through. If only a few people understand what the priorities are, the organization will struggle. But getting hundreds of people lined up behind the priorities unlocks tremendous leverage. We like to say that no one at Emerson is wandering around wondering what is expected of them. People have to know.

3. Set and Demand High Standards

A leader must have high standards for integrity, excellence, and performance. If a leader does not set high standards and observe them personally, the organization won't meet them. Compromises can be demotivating and debilitating.

Good leaders maintain a healthy level of productive tension. This does not mean that leaders impose a threatening atmosphere where people fear for their jobs. Instead they promote the kind of tension resulting from people wanting to rise to extraordinary challenges and wanting to be held accountable. True leaders challenge their people, constantly, to do better. They ask basic questions and don't accept answers that haven't been thought through.

4. Be Tough but Fair in Dealing with People

The word *tough* is often misunderstood. In 1978, *Forbes* ran a cover story on Emerson, and in the accompanying editorial, then-editor James Michaels explored the meaning of *tough* in a business context. The dictionary's definition, he pointed out, is "having the quality of being strong or firm." "Being tough," Michaels noted, "does not imply being heartless or irresponsible."

Leaders must be tough—strong, firm—in demanding performance and accountability, just as boards of directors must be tough with CEOs and management teams. This is an

Leadership starts with a commitment to success.

area where people will quickly detect compromises and modify their behavior accordingly. This doesn't mean that leaders can be arbitrary or act too quickly in making changes. That's where being fair comes in. We don't trust managers who shoot from the hip, especially on personnel matters. You have to give people enough time to find out whether they can deliver. They must have room to fail and learn from failure. If problems persist, then it's time for a change.

5. Concentrate on Positives and Possibilities

One of the best pieces of advice I received when I joined Emerson came from a veteran board member, Maurice R. "Dude" Chambers,

goals. They don't squander their time and energy on trying to meet challenges that cannot be met or trying to undo the outcomes that can't be undone. Nothing can be gained by tilting at windmills, but a great deal can be accomplished by focused efforts to achieve the possible, even if it takes a long time.

6. Develop and Maintain a Strong Sense of Urgency

I've never run across a real problem that went away because people ignored it. It will be there tomorrow, and it's going to get worse until it is resolved. It is particularly important to address operating and people problems quickly, because they will cause the most trouble in the short term.

the facts to support the best decision. And after the decision is made, we act urgently to implement it.

7. Pay Attention to Detail

We all make mistakes, and many—perhaps most—of them result from not having all the facts. Getting as much information as possible is critical to making good decisions. That takes hard work and there are no shortcuts.

Getting the facts right is vital to Emerson's success as an acquirer. Mistakes in this area can be costly. As a result, we developed what we believe to be a due diligence process second to none.

In addition to getting as much information as you can before making a key decision, you need to recognize when you don't know what you don't know—a domain vastly greater than what you are ever likely to know. When we're not comfortable with an analysis or a decision, even if we can't explain why, we've learned to insist on doing more work.

It takes hard work and hard thinking to keep things simple.

chairman of Interco. He said, "In setting priorities, don't waste time and effort on issues than can't be influenced or problems that can't be fixed. Attack the issues where you can make a difference."

Leaders invest their time and energy in reaching ambitious but attainable

Good leaders have a bias for action. They recognize that it's better to do something than nothing. If they don't get it quite right, they'll keep trying until they do. Emerson's core beliefs and management process help instill urgency in everything we do. When we confront strategic problems, we search urgently for

8. Provide for the Possibility of Failure

Things rarely go exactly according to plan, and this is one reason we plan every year. We all want to limit and control losses, but an occasional failure is the inevitable price of innovation and learning.

An organization must find ways to motivate people to think boldly and creatively. To do this, we encourage programs and initiatives that are experimental and somewhat risky, if they are well thought out.

■

When few people understand the priorities, the organization struggles.

■

Emerson's Strategic Investment Program (SIP) provides many examples of our attitude toward opportunity and experimentation. Because we don't have a corporate R&D center and because each of the divisions operates on a tight budget, we created SIP to fund projects that division managers feel are too risky or cannot be accommodated within their budgets. SIP gives them the flexibility to try new things, and it provides Emerson with some of its best growth opportunities.

9. Be Personally Involved

Leaders have a much greater chance of doing well if they are engaged in the important issues. It's impossible

to be aloof and inspirational at the same time. Yet personal involvement is a scarce resource: no one can give wholehearted attention to a great many issues.

At Emerson, we use the concept of *loose-tight controls* to guide these decisions. We carefully identify what's important and align that with our

skills. Leaders focus tightly on some issues while delegating responsibility and following loosely on others. This individual autonomy is another characteristic of high-performing organizations.

As CEO, I chose where to invest my energy by focusing on where I could have the greatest impact on performance. By spending more than half my time in planning, I challenged division leaders to think through their plans and choose their best options. I also met their direct reports and communicated my priorities to them. These sessions became occasions of high impact and leverage. I was able to work not only with the dozens of people who reported to me but

also with the hundreds of people who reported to them.

I also personally attended to two other matters. First, I signed off on the pay and benefits package at every plant, because our cost basis depended on it. For the same reason, I looked closely at regular surveys of plant-level employees to be sure we were treating our people well. Second, I invested my time in organization planning and in making management appointments, because it is the high quality of the people at Emerson that ultimately accounts for our results.

Whatever issues are most significant, it's important to stay with them. It defeats politics in an organization. When a leader works hard and tenaciously on the most important issues, it sends a clear message to everyone. And that leaves no time for politics.

10. Have fun

If you're not having fun, you're in the wrong business or wrong career. If you don't enjoy it, it isn't likely that the people you lead and work with will enjoy it either.

Emerson experiences very low turnover in its management ranks, and a principal reason is that our people take pleasure in their work and are happy at the company.

Sometimes the fun originates in traditions meant to help us relax and put aside the daily pressures. For 30 years, we've run an annual golf tournament for our key customers called the Swat Fest. It's an elimination tournament played by some unusual rules that we make up as we go. People get eliminated for crazy, arbitrary reasons. Every year, the event produces a lot of laughs and some great stories. It's a great way for our people to bond with each other and with our customers.

More fundamentally, though, the fun comes from collaborating with people who want to do well and from winning. Maintaining our record streak of annual increases in earnings, earnings per share, and dividends per share was fun. It provided motivation and pride. There is a palpable feeling of excitement that arises when you work with smart and engaged people whose goals and commitment are the same as yours.

I've been asked how I was able to sit through 27 years of planning conferences for some component division. "How can you stand it?"

people have asked me, because this process required hundreds of intense hours for each division. But

Good leaders have a bias for action.

it was fun, because I was with people who were committed to making something better.

Charles F. Knight is chairman emeritus of Emerson. As CEO, he spearheaded Emerson's evolution from a primarily domestic producer to a technology-based global manufacturer. The company's record of increased earnings per share and increased dividends for each year of his term as CEO is among the longest for consistent performance in U.S. business history. He serves or has served on the boards of directors of a number of leading global companies, including Anheuser-Busch, Baxter International, BP, IBM, Morgan Stanley, and SBC Communications.

Moral Intelligence for Successful Leadership

Doug Lennick and Fred Kiel

When we began our research on moral intelligence in the middle 1990s, we did not expect that we were about to enter an era when the cost of not having moral values at work would be so obvious. We are still unable to accurately calculate a "return on investment" for the presence of moral values in the workplace, but it is clear that the cost of the absence of moral values and the resulting moral incompetence is indeed high. In the first few years of this millennium, market capitalization of domestically traded stocks was hammered to the tune of more than $1 trillion—and a good portion of this can be attributed to the loss of confidence and trust in the honesty and integrity of our free market system.

What Is Moral Intelligence?

Moral intelligence differs from our cognitive, technical, and emotional intelligences. Moral intelligence is our mental capacity to determine how universal human principles (such as integrity, responsibility, compassion, and forgiveness—universal human principles that cut across the globe and are not gender, ethnic, culture, or religion specific) should be applied to our personal values, goals, and actions.

Recent neuroscientific advances in mapping the brain provide strong evidence that we are indeed born to be moral. We appear to have been provided with "moral hardwiring" at birth. In other words, we were born to be moral just like we were born to be lingual. We are not born knowing how to talk and we are not born moral, but we are born to speak and to develop a moral compass. Learning a language requires both the nature to learn language and the nurture of those speaking around us. Our moral intelligence is nurtured in the early years by our family or caregivers, and later in life the workplace itself serves as an arena where our moral intelligence comes into play.

Our research for our book, *Moral Intelligence: Enhancing Business Performance and Leadership Success*, strongly indicates that sustainable personal and organizational success requires moral competence, which is the active application of our moral intelligence. Moral competence is an outgrowth of "living in alignment," the interconnection of an individual's moral compass (basic moral principles, values, and beliefs) and goals, along with behaviors, including thoughts, emotions, and external actions. Living in alignment means that someone's behavior is consistent with their goals and that their goals are consistent with their moral compass. Living in alignment is not accidental. It requires understanding and building on each component while maintaining alignment among all components.

Our moral competence can indeed be enhanced throughout life. Competence shows up in behavior. And when it comes to moral behavior in

the workplace, organizations can and must create environments within which integrity, responsibility, compassion, and forgiveness—the principles of moral intelligence—come to life.

Is There Such a Thing as a Morally Intelligent Organization?

A morally intelligent organization is one whose culture is infused with worthwhile values and whose members consistently act in ways aligned with those values. A morally intelligent organization's major characteristic is that it is populated with morally intelligent people.

Organizational culture is a function of selection and leadership. As Jim Collins suggests in *Good to Great*, who is on the bus does matter! And, not surprisingly, how leaders lead matters as well.

What Collins discovered in his research is consistent with what we discovered in ours. He found what leaders believe (that is, what's embedded in their moral compasses) has a real impact on business results. He also found that leaders who go from good to great were similar in important ways. In a recent speech at a major American Bankers Association Convention, Collins noted that great leaders are both humble and ambitious. However, their ambition is for the cause, for the purpose, for the mission, not for themselves. He calls these people "Level 5 leaders" and notes they are driven to produce results but in a morally intelligent way.

Collins says this in his book: "Our research exposed Level 5 as a key component inside the black box of what it takes to shift a *company* from good to great. Yet inside that black box is yet another black box— namely, the inner development of a *person* to Level 5. We could speculate on what might be inside that

We are born to speak and we are born to be moral.

black box, but it would mostly be just that—speculation. So, in short, Level 5 is a very satisfying idea, a powerful idea, and, to produce the best transitions from good to great, perhaps an essential idea."

We do believe it is an essential idea. We also believe organizations *can, should,* and *must* do something about it. We have some ideas of our own which might help you get inside your black box.

How to Develop and Nurture Moral Intelligence in Yourself and the Workplace

Our suggestions for developing moral intelligence begin with the following understanding of leadership:

- Effective leadership of others begins with effective management of oneself.

- Effective management of oneself begins with self-awareness and ends with living in alignment.

- Living in alignment is all about aligning personal reality (thought, emotion, action) with organizational and individual goals and with the ideals represented in our moral compass (principles, values, beliefs).

In other words, effective leadership starts with self-awareness. Who are you ideally? Who are you really? What are your goals? What are your strengths? What are your gaps? What do you need to learn and what behaviors do you need to change?

Who are you ideally? If you haven't done so, we suggest you complete a personal values exercise (if you don't have one readily available to you, visit www.moralcompass.com to use ours at no cost). Also, if you don't now do so, we suggest you discuss personal values in the hiring process.

When you're deciding who you want on *your* bus you should be very interested in the personal values of the proposed riders.

Reflecting on your personal values can help build a trusting and trustworthy culture through a three-step process:

- Self-awareness. (What are your values?)
- Self-disclosure. (Share your values with your direct reports.)
- Discovery of others. (Discover the values of those who report to you.)

Within your ideals you will see your moral intelligence. Within the ideals of others, you will see their moral intelligence. As you reflect on your top five or six values, you will notice your values will be like a fabric with different kinds of fibers embedded within it. Some of the fibers will be moral, some social, some professional, and so on. Incidentally, if you examine your company values, you will discover a fabric made of similar kinds of fibers.

Who are you really? Personal reality is the moment-to-moment experience of *thought, emotion, and action (both voluntary and involuntary action)* that is constantly changing. For the most part, our personal reality can be managed through exercising the power of personal choice. Although we cannot choose our emotions and our involuntary biological processes, we can choose what to think, what to think about, and how to think about it. We can also choose what we do and what we say.

■

Great leaders are both humble and ambitious.

■

To enhance your awareness of your personal reality, which will lead directly to enhanced self-management and in turn to more effective leadership and relationships with others, we recommend you play the *freeze game* several times every day for the rest of your life.

What is the *freeze game* and how does one play it?

- At any given moment hit the pause button and check in on your personal reality. At that moment, what were you thinking? What were you feeling? What were your actions? Awareness of actions includes awareness of facial expression, body language, and tone of voice.

- Ask yourself, "Is my reality of experience aligned?" This is a two-part question: Are my thoughts, emotions, and actions aligned with one another, and is that reality of experience aligned with my goals and my moral compass?

If your reality is aligned, you are in the moment! You are in the zone! You are appropriately focused! If your reality is misaligned, you can change it. You can change what you think. You can change the tone in your voice and the look on your face. You can change what you do. Remarkably, when you change what you think and do, you will influence the emotions you feel and your involuntary biological and physical processes.

Whether you are in alignment or not, it is important to recognize you are always influencing those around you, and influencing others is what leadership is all about.

Connecting Personal Reality and Ideality with the Moral Principles of Integrity, Responsibility, Compassion, and Forgiveness

Because, as our friend the author Larry Wilson points out, we are all FHBs (fallible human beings), perfection will escape us. We might very well embrace the principles, which will mean we are indeed morally intelligent, but from time to time we will not live up to them. In those moments we will be morally intelligent and morally incompetent simultaneously.

Fortunately, however, we can enhance our ability to honor the principles by focusing on enhancing competencies related to the principles. We have identified ten competencies which support the principles. The principles and their competencies are:

Integrity	Acting consistently with principles, values, and belief
	Telling the truth
	Standing up for what is right
	Keeping promises
Responsibility	Taking responsibility for personal choices
	Admitting mistakes and failures
	Embracing responsibility for serving others
Compassion	Actively caring about others
Forgiveness	Letting go of one's own mistakes
	Letting go of others' mistakes

Improving our moral competencies results in better use of our moral intelligence. By becoming aware of who we are ideally and who we are really we can ask ourselves the following questions:

- Are my personal values in harmony or in conflict with the moral principles? If so, I have a functional moral compass. If not, I must reexamine my values and fix my compass.

- Are my goals in alignment with my moral compass? If not, I must adjust them until they are.

- Are my behaviors in alignment with my goals and my moral compass? If not, I must change my behaviors. That will require that I change my thoughts.

It is imperative to recognize we cannot choose the moral principles. They exist independent of our acceptance of them. Also, we cannot choose our emotions. What we can choose are our values, our beliefs, our goals, our thoughts, and our actions. If necessary, we can choose to change all or any of those to better align with the principles.

Conclusion

Moral intelligence, although not moral perfection, is alive and well in vast numbers of large and small companies. It is critical for sustained personal and organizational success, and the application of moral intelligence can and must be nurtured in your life and in your organization.

Doug Lennick is managing partner of the Lennick Aberman Group. Previously he led the retail distribution business of American Express Financial Advisors, and he continues to work directly with American Express Company's CEO, focusing on workforce culture and performance. His books include "The Simple Genius (You)" and "How to Get What You Want and Remain True to Yourself." His latest book, with Fred Kiel, "Moral Intelligence: Enhancing Business Performance and Leadership Success," has just been released.

Fred Kiel is co-founder of KRW International, Inc., and brings more than 30 years of experience to his work with Fortune 500 CEOs and senior executives. His focus is building organizational effectiveness through leadership excellence and aligning organizations with their vision and mission. Before founding KRW, Kiel worked with senior executives in private practice and served on the adjunct staff of the Center for Creative Leadership.

Reversing America's Corporate Brain Drain

David Heenan

For years, immigrants provided a constant pipeline of brainpower to the United States. From Alfred Hitchcock to Albert Einstein, a steady stream of energetic and highly skilled newcomers yearning to breathe free propelled America's ascendancy. Today, the country continues to benefit enormously by being a magnet for inventive and ambitious people who stimulate the economy, create wealth, and improve overall living standards. Chinese and Indian immigrants run nearly a third of Silicon Valley's high-tech firms. Eight of the 11 Americans who shared Nobel prizes in physics and chemistry in the past seven years were born elsewhere. Nearly 40 percent of MIT graduate students are from abroad. More than half of all Ph.D.'s working here are foreign-born, as are 45 percent of physicists, computer scientists, and mathematicians. One-third of all physics teachers and one-quarter of all women doctors immigrated to this country.

However, the United States can no longer live off its transplanted foreigners. Beginning in the 1990s, as their native countries improved economically and politically, many of America's best and brightest began hotfooting it home in search of another promised land.

And, as a leader, you should be worried. "We are losing our lead every day," warns Andrew S. Grove, the Hungarian émigré who co-founded Intel and made Silicon Valley all but synonymous with the entrepreneurial spirit that drives the Innovation Economy. "The distance between us and the rest of the world is eroding every day, because knowledge doesn't stay confined and people don't stay confined." For many years, the United States benefited from minimal competition in stockpiling talent. But in the ebb and flow of globalization, attractive alternatives are available elsewhere.

The New Trade Deficit in Brainpower

A decade ago, Edward Tian said good-bye to Lubbock, Texas, his pickup truck, horseback riding, and seven years of studying brown snakeweed to return to Beijing. He took home a Texas Tech doctorate in ecology and a small Internet software company he co-founded in Dallas. That business, NASDAQ-listed AsiaInfo, went on to become China's premier systems-integration company, creating as much as 70 percent of China's Internet infrastructure. "I wanted to do something to change people's lives in the next 5 years, not the next 200 years," says the 41-year-old entrepreneur. (On the heels of AsiaInfo's success, Tian went off to found telecom giant China Netcom, where he serves as chief executive.)

After centuries of importing brainpower, the United States is now a net exporter. For the past few years, nearly 200,000 foreign-born Americans—many of them, like Dr. Tian, highly talented techies—have returned to their motherlands every year. This reverse brain drain, or "flight capital," stimulated in part by lucrative government incentives, has spawned flourishing new scientific havens from South Asia to Scandinavia.

Given recent history, it was perhaps inevitable that the land of opportunity would turn its back on newcomers. In the aftermath of the terrorist attacks of September 11, 2001, more and more Americans have sought to pull up the drawbridge. U.S. Citizenship and Immigration Services has issued fewer temporary H1-B work and student visas and applied much stiffer requirements for newcomers. Talk radio and television news pundits are on a round-the-clock anti-immigrant rant, feeding ratings and fueling resentment for these "strangers" in our midst. And companies—concerned that it will appear that they are hiring foreigners instead of qualified Americans, or reluctant to deal with the maze of immigration rules, regulations, and red tape—are quietly closing the door to foreign workers, no matter how talented they may be.

But this anti-immigrant sentiment could not have come at a worse time. Survey after survey reveals that the United States faces a massive labor shortage, particularly for knowledge-oriented workers. The same is true for Germany, Japan, and the other industrial powers. On its present course, our nation of immigrants is on the verge of becoming a nation of emigrants.

■

Knowledge and people don't stay confined.

■

Credit Taiwan for inciting the exodus. With the creation of its Hsinchu Science Park in the 1980s, the Republic of China began cashing in on the knowledge-economy sweepstakes, recruiting hundreds of Taiwan-born engineers and scientists with valuable skills, experience, and contacts from the United States. Located near top universities and government research institutes and offering low-cost land, green vistas, and a minimum of bureaucracy, the Silicon Valley–style technology park helped spur a high-tech gold rush, building a critical mass of repatriated "brainiacs." Roughly one-third of the 384 companies that call Hsinchu Science Park home were founded by returnees from America. One of the first recruits was Stanford-educated Miin Wu, who in turn enticed a group of 28 Taiwanese homeboys to launch Macronix International Co.,

Ltd., in Hsinchu. "When I was at Intel, I dreamed of starting my own company," recalls Wu. "Here we mix a U.S. technology base with Taiwanese manufacturing technology." Today, the manufacturer of high-end computer chips boasts a stock market capitalization of $2 billion.

Following the footsteps of the Taiwanese, Singapore also is rolling out the red carpet to foreign scientists and entrepreneurs. One highly prized globetrotter is Hong Kong–born Edison Liu, former director of clinical sciences at the U.S. National Cancer Institute, who was wooed to head the glitzy Singapore Genome Institute. "It's a little like surfing—you see a great wave and you paddle like crazy to catch it," says Liu of his new employer. "What they have done in coordinating investment, immigration, education, infrastructure, and medical systems has been masterful. It's the most astounding social engineering I've seen in my life."

Even Vietnam is trying to entice its transplanted talent. For years, its nearly 2.7 million emigrants—a community half the size of Ho Chi Minh City—were called Viet Kieu, or "overseas Vietnamese." More than half—1.5 million—live in the United States. In the early 1990s, they started to trickle back to check out the new, more liberalized Vietnam. Now the trickle has become a flood, up to 300,000 a year, many of them returning permanently.

One prodigal son is David Thai, a 29-year-old Californian who left his homeland in 1972. After graduating from the University of Washington, he revisited Vietnam with $700 to look for an opportunity. Today, Thai runs a successful string of coffee shops in Hanoi and has investments in a coffee plantation and a coffee-export business. With its darker years behind it, the Communist-controlled government is pulling out all stops to make other *Viet Kieu* feel welcome, including posting jobs on VietnamExpress and VietnamWorks, Web sites directed at overseas Vietnamese. Vietnam is even making a major push to turn itself into an outsourcing powerhouse. One wonders: What would Ho Chi Minh think?

Turning Up the Heat

But this recruiting full-court press is not limited only to transplants from their own countries. Many countries also are intensifying their courtship of homegrown Americans. And more than a few Americans are responding to the attention. One Yankee catching the wanderlust is Norman Prouty. The 60-ish executive arrived in Bangalore in 1992 to provide venture capital to high-tech entrepreneurs in India's "Silicon Plateau." The Yale graduate worked

for 35 years in senior financial jobs at Citibank and Lazard Frères. Rather than retire, he brought a lifetime of powerful contacts and business acumen to the capital-starved country. Why India? It houses the world's largest English-speaking population outside the United States. Since most software engineering is done in English, this is a major advantage. In addition, the world's second-most-populous nation has 4 million scientific and technical professionals, including thousands who hold American doctorates.

Already, Prouty's company, ICF Ventures, has done dozens of deals to fund Indian start-ups. "Our funds come from some of the United States' most successful investment bankers, venture capitalists and institutions," says the transplanted expat. "These people have ridden some very fast horses in the U.S., and in India they see the opportunity to ride even faster ones."

For Sandra "Sam" Gershenfield, a slower, not faster, pace was the watchword. When terrorists flew two airplanes right into the place where she was working as a top

business consultant, she headed straight for the safest spot she could think of: New Zealand. "The U.S. had just become so unsafe and scary," she says from her new digs north of Auckland. "I'm so incredibly grateful to be here. If I had to describe this experience in one sentence, it's this: I found peace."

What Leaders Can Do to Reverse the Brain Drain

Leaders find themselves between Scylla and Charybdis. They have two choices: Develop more home-grown talent, or attract and retain more talented workers from abroad. The first option is unlikely to produce results in the short term; not only do business leaders have little control over America's public school system but, even if they did, such efforts would take decades to bear fruit. Therefore, leaders will have to take steps to attract and retain more immigrants in their companies, while holding on

■

Our nation of immigrants is on the verge of becoming a nation of emigrants.

■

to the existing pool of native- and foreign-born brainpower. Simply put, American business can no longer afford to see its human capital voluntarily abandon ship.

What can leaders do? Fortunately, a lot.

Know the Competition

Welcome to the brave new world, a world in which the fulcrum of international wealth and power is shifting away from the United States. Every American in a position of leadership—from business to government to academia—should travel to China or India to get a firsthand glimpse of the remarkable rise of our global competitors. They should also look beyond the highly publicized tiger economies to see how the powerful new cubs on the block—"nanonations" such as Iceland and Singapore—are striking it big in locales once removed from the world's affairs.

Adapt—or Die

Outsourcing has become the bogeyman of our times. "Outsourcing is a phenomenon that's not going to stop," says Arjuna Mahenchan, chief economist at Credit Suisse private bank in Singapore. Tactically, it's like fighting a war of attrition. If the American companies abstain from outsourcing, business will migrate elsewhere. That's how a global economy works. Rather than resist the realities—no company can afford to deprive itself of low-cost, high-skilled workers—why not exploit them? The answer lies in adaptation, not stagnation—coming up with strategies that breathe life back into the U.S. economy, from reinvesting in new jobs and industries to strengthening the safety net for displaced workers with comprehensive retraining programs.

> **American business can no longer afford to see its human capital abandon ship.**

Advocate Immigration Reform

In the post-9/11 world, America has yet to find the right balance between openness and caution—an issue in which U.S. business leaders must get involved. The *Chicago Tribune* has described our stringent immigration system as a "Tower of Babel—a cacophony of contradictory laws, strategies, and messages that ill serve the interest of the U.S. or the immigrants." No one denies the importance of improved border controls. Yet tens of thousands of gifted foreigners who want to work and study in America are entangled in shortsighted rules, regulations, and red tape. Business and government leaders must team up and take action, starting by expediting the visa process—now a drawn-out and often tortuous experience—and facilitating long-term privileges for individuals not deemed a security risk.

Dust Off the Welcome Mat

In Greek, "hospitality" is *filoxenia*—or love of the foreigner. That ancient virtue is in short supply these days—particularly due to the current anti-immigration movement. First impressions count, so America should put a stop to the traffic-cop mentality of its immigration and customs personnel. And, while it's at it, why not scrap the frosty moniker of *alien*—officially, "resident alien"—and adopt something kinder and gentler, like "honorary citizen." Rebranding Fortress America is essential if the country is to reestablish itself as the Promised Land. As the *Wall Street Journal*'s William McGurn once pointed out, "The country owes more to Ellis Island than the *Mayflower.*" Business leaders can exert a powerful influence on this attitudinal change by speaking out for an America that welcomes talented foreign workers with open arms rather than branding them as outsiders or potential terrorists.

Target the Best Minds

In the race for gifted minds, many countries are scoring great gains. America isn't one of them. On an annual basis, the United States doles out fewer than 100,000 H1-B visas for professionals and skilled workers—less than 0.4 percent of the

Rebranding Fortress America is essential.

total population. Meanwhile, America's share of international students is on a sharp decline. The United States must increase the visas reserved for knowledge workers to 50 percent—up from a mere 20 percent—and attract foreign students by making both visas and financial aid easier to obtain. Encourage your congress-people and senators to make it easier for talented knowledge workers to obtain visas to work in our country, and encourage colleges and universities to actively seek out the most gifted students.

We cannot afford to equivocate. Says the National Science Board, "Even if action were taken today, the reversal is ten to twenty years away." History offers many examples of great countries that came to catastrophic ends because of their unwillingness to respond to change. Nothing short of meeting this threat will safeguard America's talent base and shape the kind of society in which our children and their children will prosper.

David Heenan is a leading expert on globalization and author of "Flight Capital: The Alarming Exodus of America's Best and Brightest." His career in business and academia has taken him from Citigroup and Jardine Matheson to the B-schools at Wharton and Columbia. Today he serves as a trustee for the Estate of James Campbell, one of the nation's largest landowners, with assets of more than $2 billion.

Inside-Outside
Leadership for Exponential
Growth

BY DAVID G. THOMSON

H ow can you turn a Big Idea into a billion-dollar business? Of all the American companies that made an initial public offering in the past 25 years, only 5 percent achieved $1 billion in revenue—while more than 25 percent went out of business. We all chase the dream of growth, but very few achieve remarkable success. Is there a particular success pattern that these few companies followed? As a line executive, I believed there had to be a useful set of benchmarks, guideposts to manage growth by. But as I searched I found no quantitative study of the success pattern for turning a Big Idea into a stand-alone billion-dollar business. This launched a study to reverse engineer the success-based blueprint of these billion-dollar companies, which I call *Blueprint Companies*. (See the sidebar Blueprint Research on page 24.)

While Blueprint Companies represent 5 percent of the American companies that went public since 1980, the big surprise is their disproportionate impact: They account for 56 percent of employment in 2005 and 64 percent of market value created! The disproportionate success of the Blueprint Companies makes it apparent that they are the heart of America's innovation and growth. Look around and you will find Blueprint Companies everywhere. Their products enhance our everyday lives. When was the last time you used Microsoft software, accessed the Internet (which rides on Cisco equipment), searched the Web using Google, sipped a Starbucks latte, shopped on eBay or Amazon.com, purchased products at Williams-Sonoma, Staples, or Home Depot, took medicine made by Amgen, Genentech, or MedImmune, used financial services from Charles Schwab, or rode your Harley-Davidson motorcycle?

You may think every company is unique. And it is. But this minority have seen something about how to create a successful company that the rest of us are missing. The numbers prove it. Behind the numbers, seven essentials underpin this pattern of exponential growth. (See the sidebar The Seven Essentials of Blueprint Companies on page 26.) One of the most important of these essentials is the leadership team.

For bulk reprints of this article, please call 201-748-8771.

To get started on the journey to an actual billion, you need a value proposition, customers, and a business model. What about leadership? What kind of management does it take to propel a company from a blueprint to a billion-dollar revenue stream in a few years? If you relied on the covers of the business magazines, you might think it only takes an individual to run a Blueprint Company. This is not what my colleagues and I found. No single CEO can possibly keep all the essentials in motion without help. That may sound self-evident, yet we learned that *blueprint to a billion* management is actually significantly different from management at regular growth companies, especially in terms of the top leadership team.

Blueprint Companies need steady-handed managers, largely internally focused, who bring stability to an enterprise growing at lightning speed. These individuals exhibit control, discipline, and predictability. But such companies *also* need outward-facing leaders who are highly exploratory—particularly with business relationships and marketing opportunities. Thus Blueprint Companies need not one but a pair of leaders.

The Importance of Dynamic Duos

Among Blueprint Companies, we found that leadership was based on *dynamic duos*—two individuals who worked tightly together to build the firm from dreams to a billion dollars in revenue. Dynamic duos are the stuff of corporate legend: Sears and Roebuck, Roy and Walt Disney, Hewlett and Packard, and the like.

We learned that for the duo to be dynamic, one of them had to excel in the *outside* part of the effort—in marketing and sales. The other had to be the *insider*—keep-

David G. Thomson has been leading business growth for 20 years in general management and executive sales and marketing roles at Nortel Networks and Hewlett-Packard. His book "Blueprint to a Billion: 7 Essentials to Achieve Exponential Growth" is the first quantitative dissection of how America's most successful companies made it to the top.

ing the operations purring or, perhaps, inventing the better iterations of new products. Together, they had to explore and innovate continuously—whether it was in product innovation or marketing innovation. They had to make swift decisions—and quickly correct their mistakes. Most important, they had to have complete trust in and respect for one another.

The Mallett-Koogle combo at Yahoo is typical of what we found in the top Blueprint Companies: an inside-outside leadership pair, working in partnership with the founding team, who managed to execute all the essentials simultaneously. This pair, like others we have seen repeatedly in Blueprint Companies, had a unique *synergy* of talent and experience that electrified the evolution of their product, Yahoo, and its marketing. Microsoft, eBay, Nike, Starbucks, and many others have applied the same pattern, as shown by the list of dynamic duos in Table 1.

TABLE 1. INSIDE-OUTSIDE LEADERSHIP PAIRS.

Company	Leadership Pair
Yahoo	Jeff Mallett and Tim Koogle
Microsoft	Jon Shirley and Bill Gates
Tractor Supply	Jim Wright and Joe Scarlett
eBay	Maynard Webb and Margaret Whitman
Siebel Systems	Patricia House and Tom Siebel
Starbucks	Orin Smith and Howard Schultz
Broadcom	Henry Samueli and Henry Nicholas III

Blueprint Research

The research began by looking for all American companies that grew to $1 billion revenue since going public after 1980. I identified 387 companies out of 7,454. These 387 U.S. companies are referred to as the *Blueprint Companies*. The Blueprint Companies have a simple but definable characteristic: they not only grew fast, they exhibited exponential revenue growth. *Exponential growth* is super-compounding. It describes companies that can double revenue every year, for example. The non-$1 billion companies had random, linear, or no growth.

My book *Blueprint to a Billion* presents the first quantitative dissection of America's most successful growth companies. This is the first work to display the common financial pattern of America's Blueprint Companies.

These insights come from a series of research projects that took place over three years. During my research, I decided to look for patterns across industries. Is there a common set of essentials that successful companies employed across multiple industries? To answer this question, the study's problem-solving approach had parallel work streams:

1. *Financial Pattern.* The overall financial pattern of the Blueprint Companies involved a multiyear study of revenue as well as financial and shareholder-return metrics. This enabled a quantitative analysis using public data combined with real market values.

2. *Identification of the Seven Essentials.* Next, I pored through hundreds of corporate histories across multiple sectors, setting up a template that would help identify what Blueprint Companies had in common as they began their ascent to $1 billion revenue. Despite the diversity of companies and industries, I identified seven essentials that these companies had in common. The identification of these essentials led to the third work stream:

3. *Defining the Seven Essentials.* Parallel work streams were established to determine each of the essentials. My team, comprising line executives, investors, consultants, management-behavior experts, and statisticians, worked through a disciplined problem-solving process to prove or disprove hypotheses relative to each essential.

One other thing struck us: The dynamic duos who lead Blueprint Companies are not just colleagues or even just friends. They have a remarkable chemistry between them, built on a high level of respect and trust. Their relationship is dynamic in their use of complementary strengths. Their individual weaknesses are largely invisible to outside observers as they flip-flop transparently to use each other's strengths as needed. As a pair, they are the highest of high-performance teams.

With limited resources, these teams execute "1 + 1 = 3" miracles. What can we learn from them?

Three Leadership Dimensions of the Inside-Outside Leadership Duo

Blueprint leadership, it turns out, has three dimensions:

1. *Dynamic duos focus on relationships and products.* One member of the duo focuses on company-shaping relationships—that is, building relationships with marquee customers, big brother alliances, strategic investors, board members, and outsiders such as other Blueprint CEOs, suppliers, and community leaders. The other focuses on logical ideas concerned with product development, processes, and systems that fuel the company's product or service pipeline.

2. *Dynamic duos drive to innovate and explore.* While one member of the duo manages for structure, that is, problem solving for disciplined and predictable responses, the other is looking forward, exploring and shaping new opportunities. This is a delicate balance between preserving the best of the past and exploring new products and lines of business in order to innovate.

3. *Dynamic duos excel at managing the seven essentials simultaneously.* Most important, we learned the importance of management's ability to balance the execution of each of the essentials. Such a high-powered environment always involves many, many balls to juggle; it takes a particularly talented, collegial team to keep those balls in the air. Dropping one—without quickly correcting the drop—can cause a Blueprint Company to risk falling off trajectory.

Blueprint Companies have a disproportionate impact.

Qualities of Dynamic Leadership Duos

First, Blueprint leaders are superb communicators. They possess the personal chemistry, even charisma, that lets them bridge the gaps between alliance members, marquee customers, community leaders, and important investors. They are accomplished at finding, qualifying, and shaping the deals and relationships that ultimately shape the company.

One member of the leadership pair, typically the CEO, fills this role. The CEO could be an external hire, typically brought in early, or a founding member. Meg Whitman was brought in early—Microsoft's Bill Gates, Starbucks' Howard Schultz, and Nike's Phil Knight are founding members.

The role of the outside leader depends on the value proposition of the company. Nike's Phil Knight was a showcase of breakaway marketing leadership. Knight constantly pushed the boundaries—and changed the ground rules. Instead of marketing shoes, he marketed the athletes who wore the shoes and what they achieved in their Nikes.

Tom Siebel aggressively shaped marquee customer relationships with Charles Schwab and General Electric, shaped a big brother alliance with Microsoft and Andersen Consulting, and shaped his board by adding Charles Schwab and the head of Andersen as a result of an investment in Siebel.

Outside-facing CEOs actively reach out—particularly with business relationships and to create opportunities. This forward-thinking style is critical to developing marquee customers and big brother alliances, securing the right board members, and evangelizing the company's vision to employees and the community. This leader affects the forward-thinking approaches of the person whose role is focused primarily on the inside, who is usually responsible for innovation leadership.

Meanwhile, the inward-facing member of the duo exhibits control, discipline, and predictability. With this keel beneath them, Blueprint marketing and product innovators can feel secure enough to keep their vision on the cutting edge. The chief operating officer forms the inside complement to the outside-facing CEO, standing at the outside-facing CEO's right hand. Operational leaders need to be centered and well balanced. Often, they work so far behind the scenes that you hardly hear about them in the business press or notice them when you walk in the door of a company. They are adept at creating trust-based relationships and exhibit a high propensity for effective and efficient problem solving. They are real partners. If you can envision a high-performance team, this would be it.

The Number-One Inside-Outside Pair of the 1980s

Today, people often think of the prototypical inside-outside pair as Steve Ballmer and Bill Gates. But

The Seven Essentials of Blueprint Companies

1. Create and Sustain a Breakthrough Value Proposition

A value proposition states the benefits customers receive from using a company's products or services in terms that the customer understands. The best Blueprint Companies not only created but sustained breakthrough value propositions.

2. Exploit a High-Growth Market Segment

Opportunities exist in a lot of industries. Some industries have more opportunities than others. However, industries such as specialty stores generated the highest number of Blueprint Companies with 18 firms: Autozone, Staples, Tractor Supply, Williams-Sonoma, PETS-MART, and others. This occurred because there were multiple market segments to address within this industry: office supplies, teenager fashion, and pet supplies to name a few. In contrast, there are numerous cases where a single company arises out of an industry to become the only player to achieve $1 billion in revenues—witness Harley-Davidson.

3. Marquee Customers Shape the Revenue Powerhouse

Customers can be more than customers. The best of them can serve as an extension of your sales force—they become your most effective sales team! I call these *marquee customers*—that is, customers who shape the company by testing and deploying the product, recommending the company to their peers, and simply by providing exponential revenue growth on a per-customer basis.

4. Leverage Big Brother Alliances for Breaking into New Markets

The complement to marquee customers is a big brother–little brother alliance relationship. These alliances, in which a bigger company helps a smaller one, provides credibility to the little brother, gives it market in-another great example of the inside–outside dynamic can be found in the evolution of Microsoft. Back in 1983, when Microsoft was beginning to take off, the company outgrew its small-time style faster than Bill Gates could handle it. Gates had tried to take charge of five product lines. As a result, he paid little attention to tailoring programs to meet customers' needs. Key planning decisions were often delayed or not made.

Gates recognized his own shortcomings. He tried to hire a president, but the individual did not work out. He tried again in August 1983, and this time he hit gold—Jon Shirley, a 25-year career veteran at Tandy Corp., who had known Gates as a customer.

Shirley recalls, "The company lacked a lot of systems that it needed to grow, to become big. It was nothing like an ideal organizational setup and it had no MIS system. They were using a Tandy Model 2 for the general ledger." Shirley also discovered that Microsoft lacked key statistical data about its products, its markets, and its sales. "We were totally out of manufacturing space, and we had no one who knew how to run the manufacturing side," he says, looking back, adding that he threw himself into developing "a whole lot of structures and systems that would give us the tools we needed."

Analysts give Shirley credit for quarterbacking many of the key strategic alliances that helped catapult Microsoft telligence, and leads it to marquee customers. Microsoft's early alliance with IBM is a perfect example.

5. Become the Masters of Exponential Returns

A fairly common management behavior suggests that allocating more resources toward developing and introducing products will solve innovation problems. This often leads to an overinvestment situation. The technology industries serve to illustrate what it takes to create the highest value per company. They were cash-flow-positive early and sustained this positive cash flow to $1 billion revenue. Shareholder returns for being a top-performing Blueprint Company are more than compelling: an average of 87 percent returns to their shareholders while exceeding analysts' expectations 80 percent of the time!

6. The Management Team: Inside–Outside Leadership

One of the pivotal essentials that enables the others to be simultaneously executed is a dynamic leadership pairing in which one leader (or team) faces outward toward markets, customers, alliances, and the community while the other leader (or team) focuses inward so as to optimize operations. Contrary to the somewhat popular belief that one leader is *the* leader, this inside-outside leadership pair is highly prevalent among Blueprint Companies: Microsoft, eBay, Yahoo, and Tractor Supply, to name just a few.

7. The Board: Made Up of Essentials Experts

Blueprint boards are not packed with investors as one would think. Blueprint companies recruited customers, alliance partners, and other Blueprint CEOs to the board—and that makes a big difference. I call them *essentials experts* because their role is linked to the shaping and execution of one or more of the essentials. Because most investors have not scaled Blueprint Companies to $1 billion revenue, CEOs who happened to be CEOs from Blueprint Companies often were recruited to provide insight into exponential growth. In contrast, boards with only investors and management tended to be associated with struggling companies.

to industry prominence (though Shirley himself says they naturally evolved from simple customer relationships). In contrast, Gates played the market and standards leadership, shaping the technologies for various product areas. "Gates and Shirley absolutely occupied different ends of the business," says Arthur Block, Manufacturers Hanover Trust VP in charge of end-user support. "Bill focused on the IBM alliance while Jon focused on Hewlett–Packard (HP). Gates talked to user groups while Shirley talked to the financial community. Gates linked product-market opportunities to technology, while Shirley applied structure and process to the business so that it could scale."

On the day-to-day level, Shirley mirrored a management style that is supportive and didactic, well-suited to Microsoft's campus ambiance. "I believe in delegation and teaching," Shirley told *Information Week*. "You've got to give people sufficient authority to make mistakes."

Shirley retired in 1989—after Microsoft passed $800 million revenue (on the way to $1 billion the following year). He had essentially guided the company from $50 million to $1 billion as Bill Gates's "Mr. Inside."

A Leading Inside-Outside Pair Today

Tractor Supply is a wonderful case study of a similar management pair in today's management world. Tractor Supply is the number one U.S. farm and ranch store, with sales of $1.7 billion and more than 7,000 team members. The company is known for great service for its customers, full- and part-time farmers and ranchers.

*Blueprint Companies
need not one
but a pair of leaders.*

While Joe Scarlett's official title is chairman, he is more often described by those he works with as coach, cheerleader, company conscience, and chief missionary of the gospel at Tractor Supply. Scarlett provided us with a unique perspective on the dynamic duo leadership paradigm:

"Before I became chairman and my 'right hand,' Jim Wright, became president and CEO in 2004, we served as the CEO and COO team. Then and today, we are on the same page at all times. We share the same values. We finish each other's sentences. Just the other day someone remarked that we are 'like an old married couple.' The chemistry started during the interviewing process.

"When I hired Jim, we spent hours interviewing. We went to Florida and walked the stores for hours at a time. We attended a managers' meeting in Florida together. We spent two days walking through Wal-Mart, Lowe's, Home Depot, and a score of other stores, learning from them. In each of these settings we asked questions of one another, we talked strategy, we discussed values, we discussed the competition, we problem solved. We would ask each other 'how would you handle this situation?' in merchandising, operations, logistics, competition, people, and training. We got into each other's heads so well that when we are in meetings today and look at each other across the room, we often know what the other is thinking."

Managing the Seven Essentials Simultaneously

This challenge is the toughest of them all: managing all seven essentials at the same time. The inside-outside team is critical to linking the seven essentials. They determine the cross-function initiatives. More important, they balance preservation of what worked in the past with exploration for the future as the company experiences exponential growth. This is very hard to do well. Yet the leaders of our top Blueprint Companies have proven themselves to be shapers—leaders who can shape their company's destiny effectively in the face of intense uncertainty.

They are *problem solvers* and, in particular, have a comfort level for problems with a lot of moving parts. Beyond that they have a superior capacity to recognize patterns—the pattern of marquee customer behavior, the pattern of big brother alliances, patterns of linkages between the essentials, to name a few. As in a racing shell, all oars dip and swing simultaneously. The rowing team is comfortable managing scale, scope, and complexity—balanced in a single stroke.

They are also *collaborators*. They keep the team, employees, customers, partners, and investors passionate about the company's direction and execution. They develop a balanced board (as an extension of themselves for the execution of the seven essentials). In particular, they build a balanced board with members who represent the external essentials: community, customers, and alliances.

The inside-outside team is critical to linking the seven essentials.

The Bottom Line

To become a Blueprint Company leader, follow this handy leadership formula:

Blueprint Leadership = Focus on people and product
$\times$ Drive for exploration and innovation
$\times$ Ability to manage the seven essentials simultaneously

Why should you multiply the three leadership dimensions rather than add them? We found that each dimension compounds leadership effectiveness. The ideal leadership duo would create a score of $10 \times 10 \times 10 = 1,000$, rather than the 30 they'd get by addition. Alternatively, if leaders don't achieve the performance required on *each* of these dimensions, the business fails. Therefore, failing to execute any one of the leadership dimensions results in a score of zero.

Ever see a "hands-off" leader who focuses only on process with little understanding of the details of the business? Ever find leaders who are focused only on cost reduction at the expense of growth? Ever find leaders who are simply maxed-out with no time to manage all the moving parts? Not a leader for a Blueprint Company. ∎

Renewing and Sustaining Leadership

BY ANNIE MCKEE AND
RICHARD E. BOYATZIS

In recent years, we have seen a disturbing change among leaders with whom we work: they are finding it very difficult to *sustain* their effectiveness over time. Why does this happen among leaders with vision, talent, and emotional intelligence—leaders who truly understand what it takes to craft great organizations and who build healthy and transparent relationships?

Many busy executives place little value on *renewal*, or on developing practices—habits of mind, body, and behavior—that enable us to sustain ourselves in the face of unending challenges, year in and year out. In fact, it is often just the opposite. Many people and organizations confuse short-term results with long-term effectiveness and tolerate destructive behavior, discord, and mediocre leadership for a very long time. Then there are the very real pressures: increased scrutiny of financial details, omnipresent and vigilant constituencies waiting and ready to pounce, leaner organizations, and simply more work to do. Many leaders find themselves fighting just to keep their heads above water.

Power Stress and the Sacrifice Syndrome

In researching our recent book, *Resonant Leadership: Renewing Yourself and Connecting With Others Through Mindfulness, Hope, and Compassion,* we found one clue for why leaders lose effectiveness—a phenomenon that we call *power stress:* the unique brand of stress that is simply part of being a leader, especially today. For leaders today, choices are rarely crystal clear, decision making is incredibly complex, and we must influence others through ambiguous authority. Add to that the loneliness that comes with being the person at the top, and you have the formula for power stress. In the last several years, we have observed leaders experiencing power stress day after day, fighting fire after fire—and then scraping themselves off the floor each evening.

For bulk reprints of this article, please call 201-748-8771.

We have watched as these leaders became increasingly dispirited. They live with stomach problems, high blood pressure, or heart disease, or they eat and drink too much and exercise too little. Some people lose sight of everything other than their work, or the trappings of success. They lose sight of what's really important to them, even sacrificing relationships

Take the example of Niall FitzGerald, chairman of Reuters. Niall gets results—he is powerful, positive, and compelling. But it has not always been that way. For a time, Niall was caught in what we call the *Sacrifice Syndrome*. (Information presented here about Niall FitzGerald is drawn from personal conversations and correspondence with the authors.)

Niall's success was marked by meteoric rise in his career at Unilever. Over the years, he gave his all—with great results—in the service of building the business. He put the organization's needs ahead of his own and took his responsibilities very seriously. He faced challenges and threats creatively and, more often than not, successfully. Niall's life was on track and the future looked bright.

Or so it seemed. Many of us have learned (the hard way) that you do not have the kind of business success Niall had, or pursue that success as single-mindedly as he did, without it taking a huge toll somewhere in your life. The constant sacrifices and stress inherent in effective leadership can cause us to lose ourselves and strain relationships at work, at home, or both.

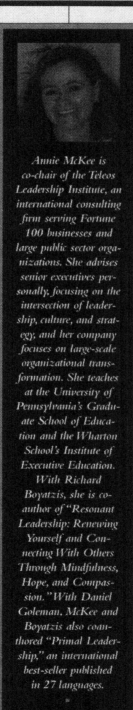

Annie McKee is co-chair of the Teleos Leadership Institute, an international consulting firm serving Fortune 100 businesses and large public sector organizations. She advises senior executives personally, focusing on the intersection of leadership, culture, and strategy, and her company focuses on large-scale organizational transformation. She teaches at the University of Pennsylvania's Graduate School of Education and the Wharton School's Institute of Executive Education. With Richard Boyatzis, she is co-author of "Resonant Leadership: Renewing Yourself and Connecting With Others Through Mindfulness, Hope, and Compassion." With Daniel Goleman, McKee and Boyatzis also coauthored "Primal Leadership," an international best-seller published in 27 languages.

For Niall, the result of the situations at home and at work was extreme pressure. Niall attempted to deal with it, of course, and for the most part he continued to be successful at work and to maintain things at home. He coped, as most of us do, through doing more of the same, working harder, and attempting to deny the signs that he was facing real problems. Ultimately, though, coping mechanisms ceased to work very well. Niall had become trapped in the Sacrifice Syndrome.

The Sacrifice Syndrome shuts down our ability to see possibilities because the effects of anxiety, fear, nervousness, and the physical damage to our brains are very real. So it was for Niall, and his first response was to deny most of the problems, on both the work and personal fronts. And although Niall tried to revitalize himself through vacations and the like, he was beyond tired. He was exhausted, and it was beginning to show in the decisions he made.

At one point, while directing Unilever's businesses, Niall and his team launched a new and seemingly revolutionary laundry product. It looked great on paper and the marketing campaign was nothing short of brilliant. Championing this product was an oasis for Niall and a wonderful escape from his growing unhappiness.

At first, things seemed fine. The product was welcomed by the market, the numbers looked great, and everyone was very excited. Then, a few warning signs popped up: there were more than the usual number of complaints about the soap; employees who tried it reported that it seemed to be harsh and that it was actually damaging their clothes. For months Niall led his team in a fight against what he thought was bad press brought on by the competition's dirty tricks.

For Niall, that first wake-up call—trouble in the business—was drawn-out and painful. Even as Niall began to recognize that the situation was serious, he continued to ignore some of the signs that his leadership was slipping. This is common. Many leaders—especially strong leaders—just don't get the truth from the people around them. This dynamic (called CEO disease) is magnified when leaders seem distant and unreachable, making even business discussions difficult.

When the product failed, Niall looked around for support and found that many of his friends had disappeared. The turmoil in his personal life had hit the boiling point as well and people who had supported him for years simply stopped calling. This was a big shock; it had never occurred to him that people would abandon him when the going got tough.

Then Niall had an extraordinary experience that finally, once and for all, woke him up. His best friend, Peter, had become very ill and had moved back to London. Despite his busy life and the stress of his current situation, the two friends spent many hours together during the long months of Peter's illness. One night as the two friends talked, Niall found himself asking, "Peter, are you afraid of death? Are you afraid of what is to come?" Neither man had any way of knowing it, but it happened that this would be Peter's last night on earth.

Richard E. Boyatzis is a professor in the Department of Organizational Behavior at the Weatherhead School of Management and Psychology at Case Western Reserve University and a visiting professor at ESADE in Barcelona. Previously, he was CEO of McBer and Company, a human resources consulting firm, and COO of Yankelovich, Skelly & White, a market research company. He is the author of more than 125 articles on behavior change, leadership, competencies, and emotional intelligence. His books include "The Competent Manager," "Transforming Qualitative Information," and "Innovations in Professional Education: Steps on a Journey from Teaching to Learning" (with Scott Cowen and David Kolb).

Peter answered that indeed he was not at all afraid, because he had made peace with himself. Then, Peter turned to Niall and said, "I have finally come to realize that what they say is *true*: life is not a rehearsal. This is all we have, this is it. I have realized this too late, and I have had to find peace with this. But it is not too late for you. You are not living the life you want to—not in your personal life, not in your work. If this is not the life you want to live, then you *must* change it. You must promise me, you owe it to me to take this realization of mine and act on it."

Peter's words shook Niall to the core. Peter was right. In that moment, Niall looked at what he most values—integrity, authentic relationships, and intimacy, and he committed to putting them first, once again.

He describes this awakening as a huge release. He was opening up to reality—first, the reality within himself, including his emotions, honest reflections about his life, and the toll his current situation was taking on his mind, body, heart, and spirit. He also saw how his decisions at work and with his family and friends had contributed to broken personal and professional relationships. As he became more aware, he found he could direct his attention more consciously, and he began seeking real solutions instead of Band-Aids and compromises. He began to see things that he had missed for many years, giving him deeper insight, more choices, and the beginning of wisdom.

Waking Up to Renewal

We have seen many leaders who, arriving at the point that Niall had reached, simply rationalize or ignore all signs of problems and numb themselves to the consequences of their actions. In fact, this is common. Many leaders experience a slow, steady decline in effectiveness, health, and happiness. It happens over many years, simply as a result of the constant pressures and the need to give so much of oneself. The trouble is, the subtle messages that tell us something is not right are often just whispers. It is easy to miss them. Then, one day, we find ourselves waking up to the fact that we are worn out, tired, or just unable to give anymore—simply burned out.

But some people, like Niall, hear and recognize wake-up calls. These calls can be a first critical step to dealing with the Sacrifice Syndrome. Niall ultimately realized that he needed more than just rest and relaxation. He needed *renewal* to sustain himself. The effects of chronic power stress do not allow the mind, body, or heart to flourish, and as a consequence even the spirit may wane. When we engage in personal renewal, we are better equipped to deal with the challenges and sacrifices inherent in leadership. Let's look at why this works.

Recent research shows that renewal invokes a brain pattern and hormones that change our mood, while returning our bodies to a healthy state. This sets into motion a chain reaction that evokes changes in perception and eventually in behavior. Renewal begins as certain experiences arouse a different part of our limbic brain from the one involved in stress responses. This in turn stimulates neural circuits that increase electrical activity in our left prefrontal cortex, leading to arousal of the body's parasympathetic nervous system (PSNS). A different set of hormones is released into the bloodstream than when the sympathetic nervous system (SNS) is aroused. These activate another set of hormones that lower blood pressure and strengthen the immune system. A person then feels a sense of well-being—elated, happy, and optimistic. Once in this emotional state, we are more likely to perceive events as positive rather than negative or threatening, further enhancing the condition that we call *renewal*.

The experiences of mindfulness, hope, and compassion foster and provoke arousal of the PSNS and the condition of renewal. A positive cycle is triggered: being in renewal feeds hope, compassion, and mindfulness while it counters the detrimental effects of stress. Therefore, sustainable, effective leadership occurs only when we wake up and ensure that the sacrifice and stress of leadership are interchanged with experiences of renewal.

> *The Sacrifice Syndrome shuts down our ability to see possibilities.*

Mindfulness, Hope, and Compassion

How did Niall turn things around and begin the process of renewal? To counter the Sacrifice Syndrome, he needed to make renewal a way of life. This requires conscious action and, for most people, intentional change. We have seen, and the research supports our observations, that there are actually concrete ways to achieve renewal. Specifically, renewal involves three experiences—*mindfulness, hope, and compassion*—that we can, with practice, cultivate as a way of life.

Mindfulness

The first element is *mindfulness,* or living in a state of full, conscious awareness of one's whole self, other people, and the context in which we live and work. We define mindfulness as *being awake, aware, and attending*—to ourselves and to the world around us. Mindfulness enables us to pay attention to what is happening to us, and to stop the Sacrifice Syndrome before it stops us.

People who cultivate mindfulness have more cognitive flexibility, creativity, and problem-solving skills. In other words, leaders who pay attention to the whole self—mind, body, heart, and spirit—can literally be quicker, smarter, happier, and more effective than those who focus too narrowly on short-term success.

To return to Niall: part of the reason for his success was that he *has* the capacity for mindfulness. The problem was, as the pressure increased and as a result of becoming more powerful, he had let his attention to himself and others slip. So, for Niall, the question was, "How can I reengage my capacity for mindfulness?"

He started with a lot of reflection. He built in time to think—and to concentrate on getting clear about what he was feeling and what he was doing. He often did this while running, so the effects of exercise helped him to think clearly while he also took care of his health. He also reached out to one or two people and used them as sounding boards to check on his reflections. He took the risk of being vulnerable with his closest friends—admitting that maybe he was making mistakes that

needed fixing (at work and at home), and he asked for opinions and help.

Hope

The second element, *hope,* enables us to believe that the future we envision is attainable, and to move toward our visions and goals while inspiring others toward those goals as well. In fact, the experience of *hope* actually causes changes in our brains and hormones that allow us to renew our minds, bodies, and hearts. When we experience hope, we feel excited about a possible future, and we generally believe that the future we envision is attainable. Hope engages and raises our spirit, mobilizes energy, and increases resiliency. Beyond this, hope and the vision of the future that comes with it are contagious. They are powerful drivers of *others'* behavior. Hope is an emotional magnet—it keeps people going even in the midst of challenges.

> *To counter the Sacrifice Syndrome, make renewal a way of life.*

In Niall's case, hope was in short supply for a while. At Unilever, the laundry product situation looked bad and it would have been easy for Niall, and then the team, to sink into despair. But two things stopped this slide. First, Unilever's leaders did not lose faith in Niall. Then, as Niall took control—and responsibility—for the situation, he found energy to direct the team's efforts toward the future. Let's look at how this played out.

Even during the worst days of the debacle, Unilever's leadership still believed that Niall could become the next chairman. This both surprised and pleased him, as it was a dream he had had for many years. So even at the low point, he could see a more positive future. This gave Niall strength to seriously question his decisions during the product launch. He looked at this situation from different perspectives and let go of the single-mindedness that had characterized his treatment of the problem. He took responsibility, deciding to stay with the business and see it through. He could easily have gotten out of it, moved on, and let someone else clean things up. But instead he asked Unilever's board for permission to stay in the business, to see it through until things began to turn around.

Niall's hopeful view of the future and his actions inspired commitment and ultimately sparked renewal on the team. The image of the future that Niall generated was realistic—difficult, but possible. As Niall began to imagine a different—and feasible—future, his hope became contagious. At work, others began to understand and see his vision and realistic possibilities for the future.

Compassion

When we experience *compassion*, we are in tune with the people around us. We understand their wants and needs, and we are motivated to act on our feelings. Like hope, compassion invokes renewal in our mind, body, and heart. And like hope, compassion is contagious.

If asked about the years of struggle and confusion, Niall would probably have said that he felt tremendous compassion for the people in his life who were hurt by his actions at work and at home. But compassion is different from sympathy, or even empathy, in that it goes beyond understanding. Compassion is a combination of deep understanding, caring, and *willingness to act on that concern.*

Conversely, as much as we need to show compassion for renewal to take place, we also must receive it. When we are in emotional turmoil and especially when we find that some of our life's foundations are crumbling, we need to know that others care, that they are offering us their concern, compassion, and love.

Niall was lucky. Even though many friends had deserted him, a few stayed by his side. They seemed to understand that he was not just a man who had made a mess of things, he was still a truly good person and a good businessman. They saw him as someone who had made some bad choices along the way—but also as a person who could, and would, right the wrongs of the past and return to more balance. One of those people was Peter, Niall's dying friend.

> *Positive emotions enable us to remain resilient in the face of challenges.*

The dynamic relationship among mindfulness, hope, and compassion sparks the kinds of positive emotions that enable us to remain resilient in the face of challenges, even in the unprecedented climate that leaders face today. Together these elements counter the destructive effects of power stress and keep us continually in a state of renewal, and thus they help to produce strong relationships and great leadership while helping leaders and people around them renew themselves.

Personal Renewal and Professional Excellence

Niall FitzGerald is an outstanding leader, and in other, more personal roles in his life, he is living up to his own high standards. We have seen him in action—people in the business world look up to him, and he is having an impact on social causes that are close to his heart. And maybe most important, his personal life is now vibrant and happy.

For Niall, getting back in touch with his values—what he truly, deeply believes to be important—was at the center of his renewal. In his moments of greatest self-doubt and uncertainty about the future, he began to reconstruct a life of meaning from his values.

As we have seen in Niall's story, even those of us who *can* be strong leaders will at times lose our way. This is why we need to catch the Sacrifice Syndrome before it starts and do something about it. To learn how to counter the Sacrifice Syndrome and engage in renewal, most of us have *personal work* to do. We need to find our passion, take a good, hard look at who we are and the life we are leading, break old patterns, and get rid of old habits. We need to cultivate mindfulness and learn how to engage hope and compassion even (maybe especially) when we are under extreme pressure.

So What Are You Going to Do About It?

Great leaders are awake, aware, and attuned to themselves, to others, and to the world around them. They commit to their beliefs, stand strong in their values, and live full, passionate lives. Great leaders are emotionally intelligent and they are *mindful:* they seek to live in full consciousness of self, others, nature, and so-

Even those of us who can be strong leaders will at times lose our way.

ciety. Great leaders face the uncertainty of today's world with *hope:* they inspire through clarity of vision, optimism, and a profound belief in their—and their people's—ability to turn dreams into reality. Great leaders face sacrifice, difficulties, and challenges, as well as opportunities, with empathy and *compassion* for the people they lead and those they serve.

We have found that leaders who sustain their effectiveness understand that renewing oneself is a *holistic* process that involves the mind, body, heart, and spirit. But becoming a strong leader does not happen by accident. People who think they can be truly great leaders without personal transformation are fooling themselves. You cannot inspire others and create the relationships that ignite greatness in your family, organization, or community without feeling inspired yourself, and working to be the best person you can be.

So if you wonder whether you are a leader who can sustain leadership for the long term, ask yourself these questions:

- Are you inspirational?
- Do you create an overall positive emotional tone that is characterized by hope?
- Are you in touch with others? Do you know what is in others' hearts and minds? Do you experience and demonstrate compassion?
- Are you mindful—authentic and in tune with yourself, others, and the environment? ■

Passing the Torch of Leadership

BY ROBERT P. GANDOSSY
AND NIDHI VERMA

In March 2005 Robert Iger, a nine-year Disney veteran, was chosen to replace embattled Disney CEO Michael Eisner despite running against a star-studded cast of outside CEOs including eBay's Meg Whitman, Yahoo's Terry Semel, and the Gap's Paul Pressler. The appointment of an inside candidate demonstrated the board's confidence in Disney's internal talent capability.

Despite a few notable examples of companies that invest in building internal bench strength, many companies don't deal with succession management seriously because they are confident about sourcing external talent when they face a talent crisis. "Twenty years ago," says Jeff Sonnenfeld, associate dean at the Yale School of Organization and Management, "only 7 percent of the firms hired CEOs from the outside. Now it's 50 percent." Although external leadership appointments are gaining ground, experts emphasize the profound benefits of succession from within. Sourcing external candidates is not only expensive, it probably reduces the chances of success for the new leader.

Globally, over the past seven years, home-grown CEOs delivered 1.9 percentage points per year higher shareholder returns than externally appointed CEOs did, according to Booz-Allen Hamilton's annual study of CEO succession at the world's 2,500 largest companies. Further, a company's decision to recruit from outside can have a deleterious effect on its retention strategy. By hiring externally the company sends a dangerous message to its employees that they are seen as incompetent. Internal talent may feel stagnant and uninspired, and may jump ship when their hope of earning a top seat is shattered.

A study carried out by Stanford University researchers James C. Collins and Jerry I. Porras, culminating in their best-seller *Built to Last*, found that companies that maintained a stellar performance and endured through the 20th century had one essential ingredient, a culture of succession management. According to the authors, visionary companies like Procter & Gamble, General Electric, Wal-Mart, 3M, and Sony are clock builders who preserve their core by developing, promoting, and carefully selecting home-grown managerial talent. The research found that visionary companies were six times more likely than other companies to promote insiders to CEO. On the other hand, nearly 34 percent of Fortune 1,000 companies do not have a C-level succession plan, according to Drake Beam Morin, a global human capital management firm.

In the past, when the business environment was less volatile and senior leaders had longer tenures, organizations were not significantly hurt by neglecting succession management. Times have changed. With a looming shortage of top talent caused by the impending demographic time bomb, this lack of preparedness by most organizations can have crippling consequences. A 2005 study by the Corporate Leadership Council found that 72 percent of companies predict they will encounter an increasing number of leadership vacancies over the next three to five years, while 76 percent are "less than confident" in their ability to staff these positions. A top leader's departure from a company can take a heavy toll on employee engagement, business performance, and shareholder value. The crisis is magnified in the absence of any comprehensive succession strategy and program. This article presents a case for introducing or reviving a best-in-class succession management system and examines why—despite the widespread spotlight and renewed attention on succession management in recent times—only a rela-

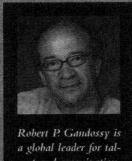

Robert P. Gandossy is a global leader for talent and organization consulting for Hewitt Associates, with expertise in improving organizational effectiveness and human resource strategy, and increasing growth through innovation. He has written more than 50 articles and 5 books and has been a speaker for a number of groups including Harvard Business School, the Human Resources Planning Society, the Wharton School, and the Tom Peters Group, to name a few.

tive handful of organizations are getting it right. The article is based on our experience with numerous clients and on Hewitt Associates' Top Companies for Leaders research, which examines the building blocks that allow financially successful companies to consistently produce a sustainable pipeline of leadership talent. Hewitt's 2005 Top Companies for Leaders study examined 373 public and private U.S. companies.

Resistance to Succession Processes

Most organizations recognize the benefit of having a carefully designed and well-executed system for passing the leadership mantle. However, they are reluctant to plan for unpleasant scenarios such as an incumbent's exit and often procrastinate and put off the process for the future. For example, even after knowing in April 2005 that Peter Jennings, the incredibly talented anchorman of ABC's *World News Tonight,* was suffering from inoperable lung cancer, the program did not identify a long-term successor, probably to avoid seeming insensitive. Having a succession plan in place would have allowed Jennings not only to have a say in the selection process but to mentor the new incumbent to step into his highly demanding and prestigious role.

Some also fear that naming a successor may cause other talented executives to leave the organization. Neville Isdell's appointment as the CEO of Coca-Cola in June 2004 created a split within the company's upper management, where some reportedly favored the candidacy of Steven Heyer, the 51-year-old former Turner marketing executive who apparently has since left the company. The leadership shuffle at Morgan Stanley in March 2005 would have probably been accepted with less uproar had there been a more focused and planned approach to succession. Amid other controversial and unpopular business decisions, beleaguered CEO Philip Purcell named two new co-presidents to usher in the "new generation of leaders." Purcell's decision seemed to be the final nail in his coffin and triggered a chain of top executive resignations among those who did not approve of his management choices.

Building Best-in-Class Succession Management

Many of these problems arise from succession programs that focus on singular "succession events." Organizations that plan only for one or two senior management departures do little more than pay lip service to succession planning—and invite succession turmoil. Organizations that embrace a formal, ongoing, top-to-bottom succession process that is a fundamental part of the corporate fabric—what we call best-in-class succession management—have developed a key ingredient for long-term success, as Collins and Porras demonstrated.

Where traditional succession planning focuses on compiling a list of possible replacements, succession management is a more holistic and strategic approach to building the internal talent force. It looks to both identify and develop high-potential leaders capable of executing the corporate strategy. *Therefore, best-in class succession management primarily involves two key activities: strategically tracking mission-critical roles that are emerging as "pressure points" and proactively sourcing and developing a strong talent pool of potential candidates to fulfill these pivotal roles.* Best-in-class

Nidhi Verma is a senior consultant in the Talent and Organization Practice in Hewitt Associates. She provides consulting and thought leadership on talent management, performance effectiveness, and change. She writes in the area of talent development and strategic directions of the human resources function. Gandossy and Verma are coeditors of the forthcoming book "Workforce Wake-Up Call: Your Workforce Is Changing, Are You?"

organizations are those that go beyond the traditional approach and focus on integrated and aligned succession processes aimed at enhancing current and future organizational capacity.

Succession Cornerstones

The success of a succession management program hinges on having a strategic, systematic, and consistent approach that develops future employee and organizational capability. Succession planning strategies range from simple replacement planning to integrated development planning. The core of developing a steady and reliable pipeline of "A" players rests on five fundamentally important cornerstones—*Alignment, Commitment, Assessment, Development, and Measurement.* Central to the success of the five cornerstones is an unflinching commitment to execution. A carefully designed succession management strategy can fail or wither on the vine because of flawed or no execution. The components of succession management systems are illustrated in Figure 1 on page 41.

Now let's begin to unpack and add some details to succession cornerstones.

Alignment

In an ever-changing business environment, companies need to strive constantly to build a reliable supply of talent, not only to fill executive vacancies but to achieve their future vision. Best-in-class organizations use succession management as a strategic business planning tool to focus on both current and future staffing needs and to develop a pool of highly talented individuals for meeting the organization's long-term strategy. These companies rely on corporate strategies to determine and drive their leadership competencies and talent development needs.

In 2005, IBM refreshed the leadership competencies it had developed in 2003 to reflect the rapidly changing environment, become more future focused, and create "on-demand leadership for an on-demand world." The company interviewed 30 senior leaders who embodied behaviors needed for IBM's future success and developed a new leadership model comprising competencies required by IBM's leaders to build an on-demand culture. For example, "dedication to client success" and "innovation that matters" were identified as two key business values. To support these values IBM defined collaboration and horizontal thinking as competencies to be displayed by its leaders.

At Johnson & Johnson, the Credo, a 60-year-old document, embodies the company's core values and outlines responsibilities toward customers, employees, community, and shareholders. It provides a foundation for understanding leadership development at J&J. Based on the values described in the Credo, J&J created the Global Standards of Leadership, a document designed to provide the organization with guidance for the development of leaders. The Standards of Leadership has the Credo at its core, with business results around it. Each spoke on the wheel—innovation, collaboration, complexity and change, organizational and people development, customer and marketplace focus—represents a management responsibility. J&J uses these standards for evaluating employees. J&J's CEO William Weldon says, "There's forgiveness on the numbers side but not on the Credo values. Business results have to be tied to them."

Real succession management is key to long-term success.

Commitment

Leaders need to go beyond paying lip service to succession management: real leadership and management buy-in, involvement, and commitment is critical.

Ongoing involvement and commitment takes several forms. First, the senior leadership should play an active role in the succession management process by driving and promoting it as a strategic imperative and leading by example. At General Electric, former CEO Jack Welch—and now Jeff Immelt—have made leadership development a top priority and have demanded that their executives follow suit. As a result, GE promotes nearly 85 percent of its leaders from within. Several of Hewitt's Top Companies reported that their board members visit the high-potentials at their locations and make a concerted effort to know them at a personal level. At one Top Company the CEO maintains a mentoring partnership program wherein he meets with early and mid-career high-potentials throughout the year.

Second, leaders should have a strict discipline to hold managers accountable for identifying and developing talent in their work area by tying it to their reward or promotion. One Top Company links 30 percent of senior leaders' compensation to talent development. Managers are assessed on how effectively they develop talent over a 12-month period and their compensation is adjusted accordingly.

Finally, adequate investment in financial and people resources for succession management will reinforce the point that the senior leadership not only believes in the impor-

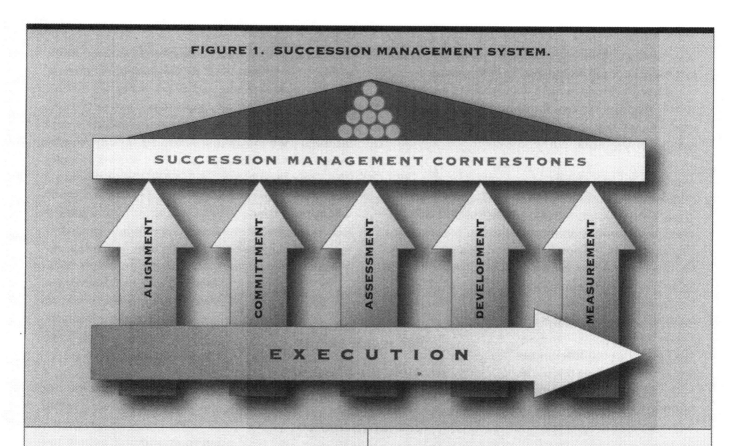

FIGURE 1. SUCCESSION MANAGEMENT SYSTEM.

SUCCESSION MANAGEMENT CORNERSTONES

ALIGNMENT COMMITTMENT ASSESSMENT DEVELOPMENT MEASUREMENT

EXECUTION

tance of succession management but undertakes necessary steps to embed it in the organization.

Identification

Assessment of mission-critical positions—jobs that are vital for the long-term performance and health of the business—and identifying and stocking pools of talented individuals to fill these positions are critical components of a succession management process. The process of assessing successors usually begins with a well-designed competency model based on the organization's strategic plans. After the core competencies are determined, a battery of methods can be employed to assess employees on these predetermined skills and competencies. Thereafter, candidates can be classified as "ready now" (can be promoted to the next level within 12 months), "ready later"

(can be promoted to the next level within a few years), "steady state" (likely to continue developing at the current level), "dark horse" (not keeping up with the requirements of the level), or "newbie" (too early to assess). This grid enables selection and classification of multiple successors or a "chain of successors" for a targeted position and can form the basis for appointing the most suitable successor when an opening occurs.

In the absence of a consistent talent review process, managers rely on subjective assessment of the candidates and base their assessment on personal and often limited impressions of the individual. Moreover, talent identification can be vague and confusing when the criteria or guidelines for assessing talent are not explicitly stated. With no prevalent criteria managers tend to wear perceptual blinders and favor people who seem to be similar to themselves, failing to respect differences in personalities and working styles. Also, managers may rely on brief observations or solitary victories. For example, they may observe someone perform well on a small project and conclude that the employee is a consistent star performer.

Too often the talent review process suffers because of its singular focus on the top echelons. Hewitt's 2005 Top Companies for Leaders research revealed that 65 percent of Top 20 Companies regularly use succession plans for middle management positions while 85 percent regularly use the process for senior management positions. A leading global chemical company focuses heavily on building capabilities of its front-line and middle management employees. The company relies on its "global skill resource managers" to manage one of the seven skill families such as process or project engineers and manufacturing control engineers.

Similarly, focusing on just the star players—employees who can be clearly and easily categorized as high-potentials—and not other solid contributors can also be restrictive. Occasionally, solid contributors—employees with scarce or unique skills, those with critical organizational knowledge, or customer relationship skills—are ignored.

Development

Long-term bench development and advancement is essential for the success of succession management. Best-in-class companies adopt development as a strategic priority and provide a range of targeted development experiences to enhance the capabilities of their future leaders for their "destination jobs." They report offering stretch assignments, internal or external training, nomination to executive programs or MBAs, mentoring, coaching, action learning, and special, enterprise-wide rotational projects. P&G develops internal leaders by moving people within countries, within regions, and around the world. "We want people in roles for three to five years so they live with their own mess," says Moheet Nagrath, P&G's vice president of HR Global Operations. Examples of developmental assignments deployed by Top 20 Companies include nominations to Six Sigma projects and appointments to boards of nonprofit organizations to accelerate high-potential development and provide opportunities to demonstrate skills beyond current job responsibilities. (For a discussion of how nonprofit board service accelerates leadership development, see "Developing Visionary Leaders" in this issue—*ed.*)

Home Depot is committed to building its internal talent bench. At every step of an employee's career, structured assessment and development programs ensure that the best talent is recognized and developed. Many new hires enter a series of rotational leadership programs—including store leadership, merchandising, business leadership, and internal audit roles. Individuals are invited to participate in the development programs after a rigorous process involving interviews, behavioral assessments, role-plays, and other exercises. There are no promotions at Home Depot without an objective assessment.

The most senior-level employees—the top 100 or so high-potentials—have intensive leadership development programs throughout the year. The Executive Leadership Program, for example, is designed for a group of 30 at Home Depot offices. During the year, members enroll

> *"We want people in roles for three to five years so they live with their own mess."*

in a three-week program focused on leadership, management issues, and enterprise-wide business challenges. Well-known faculty from across the globe are invited to help facilitate. According to Jennifer Williams, a senior director of HR, these various programs are focused on broad leadership development and are designed to encourage cross-function, cross-business interaction among the company's most promising leaders.

Intel places a premium on grooming internal talent. It practices a method called "two in a box" that allows executives to overlap job duties, learning from and supporting each other in building skills they each lack. They learn new skills while also covering areas in which they lack experience.

Many organizations jeopardize the success of their development programs by adopting a one-size-fits-all training approach. In addition, they do not assign accountability for managing and monitoring the delivery of the programs. Others limit their success by endorsing a polarized approach where they either keep the entire process within HR's bastions without involving business managers or give its full control to line managers with little or no involvement of HR. Both scenarios can spell doom. When managers are not involved in planning and sanctioning development projects for their employees, they are reluctant to champion these programs and encourage their employees to allocate time to undertake them. In the same vein, managers do not have the time or inclination to get embroiled in the tactical and administrative details of conducting developmental activities and prefer HR to guide the process, manage the infrastructure, and monitor employee follow-up in developmental activities.

Measurement

Organizations that do not invest time or resources in measuring the victories and learning from the failures of a succession management program are awaiting disaster. Measurement is twofold: assessing the effectiveness of the overall program and tracking the success of an individual placement.

Since measurement of a succession initiative can be nebulous and nonquantifiable, many companies do not even bother to establish metrics. Such companies face a higher risk of making these processes outmoded and out of touch with real business and individual succession needs, causing them to become unpopular with business managers and employees. Other organizations looking to define metrics for evaluating a succession program blunder when they force-fit an off-the-shelf measurement scorecard without calibrating and customizing it to match the needs and expectations of their company's employees and leaders. Each company should determine evaluation criteria and benchmarks based on the distinct characteristics of its own succession management program.

Model succession management programs use a variety of measures to ensure that desired outcomes are achieved, and they set targets to ensure continuous improvement. These include

• Extent to which leadership job openings can be filled from internal pools

• Average number of qualified candidates per leadership position

• Ethnic and gender diversity in promotions

• Number of positions with two or more "ready now" candidates

• Percentage of high-potentials who complete development plans

• Attrition rate from the succession pool

Further, tracking and measuring the progress and development of individuals targeted for succession is equally important. It is often said that high performance is not just about reaching the pinnacle but staying there. When companies fail to review and measure their high-potentials at regular intervals they do not realize that designated top talents may be underachieving in their new role and may have fallen out of the high-potential status. An individual's performance could be falling either because of failing to achieve expectations in the new role or because of wrong assessment by the employee's manager. One Top 20 Company formally measures the success of succession planning decisions three years after a placement.

It's All About Execution

Failure in execution may be due to the lack of an organization's willingness to execute, its ability to execute, or both. Typically, problems in execution derive from a combination of process issues and people issues.

• Process-based problems include use of a vague and ad-hoc succession management strategy that is not aligned to business strategy; complex, bureaucratic, and difficult-to-understand succession management tools and templates; unclear roles and responsibilities of different constituents (HR, leadership, business managers, and employees); frequent changes to the original process, and similar faults.

• People issues that compound the many challenges of effective execution include resistance from managers and employees, reluctance of managers and employees to commit resources and time, and managers' personal insecurities and prejudices in selecting top talent.

Companies that have effective and enduring succession management programs pay attention to and iron out both process- and people-related execution problems.

Hewitt's 2005 Top Companies for Leaders study reveals that the Top 20 Companies get more from their leadership practices by executing them effectively. For example, while 100 percent of the Top Companies and 73 percent of other companies have leadership competencies, the Top 20 Companies are significantly better at integrating these into leadership processes. All the Top 20 Companies integrate these competencies into the succession planning process, while only 78 percent of other companies do so.

Investment in the Future

A best-in-class succession management program is a well-founded answer to an impending business crisis. No business can safeguard itself against key talent departures. At some point a company's critical chairs get empty because of an incumbent's retirement, resignation, poor performance, or untimely death—pushing the organization to search for a replacement. This search can pose significant operational and financial risk if the business has not invested in building its future leadership pipeline internally.

Granted, there is a clear acknowledgment of long-term benefits from robust succession management systems, but organizations are often slow to invest in and commit to best-in-class processes. Lack of a disciplined approach toward succession management or tolerance of substandard execution can seriously injure an organization's efforts at leadership continuity, talent development, and retention of key individuals. The cornerstones described in this article are simple but often overlooked. By working intensely on planning, executing, and winning on the five succession management cornerstones, companies can develop a steady pipeline of competent successors for their targeted, mission-critical positions. ∎

Developing Visionary Leaders

BY ALICE KORNGOLD

To ensure that corporations, governments, and NGOs are headed up by effective leaders, and that our children live in a world of promise—safely, productively, peacefully, and prosperously—we need leaders with integrity, vision, and competence. How do we develop good leaders? While education plays a role, leadership is ultimately developed through experience, not in classrooms. Here lies a win-win: while businesses seek learning environments to cultivate leaders, nonprofits are in dire need of board members with business acumen—in strategy, finance, mergers, public relations, human resources, law, real estate, accounting, and other core areas. Furthermore, nonprofits need boards that are fully engaged and focused on the key strategic issues: the vision, the future, the potential, and how to achieve it.

A Unique Breeding Ground for Leadership Development

America's nonprofit organizations, numbering an estimated 1.3 million, provide health and human services, education, and arts and culture in communities nationwide. These nonprofits are facing extraordinary strategic challenges as they deal with funding cuts, changing communities, and increasing needs. The responsibility to address these challenges falls squarely on the shoulders of nonprofit boards of directors and the CEOs they hire. For nonprofits to succeed in today's tough environment, financial and strategic hurdles must be faced at the board level, in partnership with the organization's chief executive. Hence, the nonprofit boardroom has become the perfect environment for leadership development.

Businesses that want to have successful leaders in their top ranks can encourage and support the participation of their young executives in nonprofit board experiences where they can develop their fullest potential. In serving on a nonprofit board, one must look at the entire organization from above (not simply one's particular division),

For bulk reprints of this article, please call 201-748-8771.

consider the stakeholders and the mission, understand the revenue model and its vulnerabilities, identify and assess alternative models for revenues, revisit the mission and its relevance, articulate the compelling value of the organization, assess and understand community needs, identify and evaluate other service providers, determine the core services that have the greatest impact, explore strategic alliances, envision the future, build consensus, lead through persuasion, and develop and mentor newer board members. The opportunity for young executives to exercise such leadership skills on nonprofit boards is in stark contrast with their corporate roles, which are much more narrowly focused.

Nonprofit boards provide the breeding ground for businesses and communities to develop the next generation of leaders. And their imaginative achievements will bring a greater future for our neighborhoods, regions, nation, and world.

To understand the potential value of the nonprofit board experience, we must first look at the role of the board. Unfortunately, a concept of governance that is limited to mere oversight shortchanges both the nonprofit sector and the leadership development opportunity.

Beyond Oversight

Oversight, the word commonly used to describe the business of board governance, is not leadership. Certainly boards must be held accountable to exercise their three core fiduciary duties: the duty of *care*—to be attentive board members, participate in board meetings, read board materials and minutes, and be knowledgeable about the

Alice Korngold is author of "Leveraging Good Will: Strengthening Nonprofits by Engaging Businesses." She was founding president and chief executive officer of Business Volunteers Unlimited, a national model organization that trained and placed over 1,000 business executives on 275 nonprofit boards. She is a national consultant to corporations, nonprofits, and foundations, focusing on governance and leadership development. Her work has been featured in a page one article of the Wall Street Journal and in other national media.

organization, its finances, and its issues; the duty of *loyalty*—to put the organization's interests above personal and professional interests and bring any potential conflicts of interest to the board's attention; and the duty of *obedience*—to serve a mission, making all board decisions in the interest of the mission. These are serious and fundamental responsibilities.

The good news is that nonprofit boards are covering those basic elements well. According to a recent authoritative study by Lester M. Salamon and Stephanie L. Geller at the Center for Civil Society Studies Institute for Policy Studies at Johns Hopkins University, "There is solid evidence of effectively functioning boards, reasonable management and accountability practices, widespread adherence to best-practice accreditation systems, and reasonable conflict of interest and related ethical standards." Hence, in spite of a few renegades, for the most part, boards are behaving decently.

Unfortunately, given the present pressures on the nonprofits, mere oversight is inadequate to lead one of the nation's most important sectors. Nonprofit boards must do more than watch the books and stay clear of conflicts of interests.

The Duty of Imagination

Beyond the duties of care, loyalty, and obedience, there is, I suggest, a fourth board duty: the duty of *imagination*. It is imperative for boards to imagine the greater potential for the organizations they lead—to envision, create the strategic path, and provide the support for its achievement. This is leadership.

Some nonprofit boards are making the duty of imagination the norm, not the rarity. One such example is Make A Wish Foundation of America, whose mission is to "grant the wishes of children with life-threatening medical conditions to enrich the human experience with hope, strength, and joy."

As Suzanne Sutter, CEO of Things Remembered, a national chain of novelty stores, ascended to Make A Wish board leadership in 2003, she was fully aware that she was inheriting an organization in financial distress. For quite some time, a number of board members had been concerned about the organization's underperformance. They were also puzzled with the poor state of affairs given that the Make A Wish mission was so compelling and the brand was golden. In the year leading up to her board chairmanship, Suzanne was asked to head up the board's strategic action planning process. The board and leadership of the foundation engaged a national consulting firm to define the major performance issues of the entire foundation and propose strategic actions.

Beyond care, loyalty, and obedience, nonprofit boards need a duty of imagination.

Together, the leadership righted the model by building the national board and organization into the powerhouse that could establish corporate partnerships and serious funding to rain support throughout the national network. Additionally, the national board began the process of setting quality standards to ensure the value of the brand, and also end the pain of the smallest chapters by merging them into larger, more sustainable regions.

Analyzing the situation, envisioning the greater potential, and creating a strategic concept were one thing. Leading and facilitating change was another. This was a massive undertaking, and Suzanne could only accomplish this transformation by identifying and engaging a valued group of strong board members to work with her to lead the change. The key to success was selling this plan to the chapters, which would have to endorse the new organizational model by vote. In fact, this would involve the local chapters' relinquishing some of their powers with an expectation that the national board and organization would fulfill its promise of greater relevance and support.

Essentially, what the board diagnosed was an organizational upside-down cake. The national organization had been dependent on its network of local members, often small grassroots chapters in communities with failing economies, to feed the beast bottom-up. Furthermore, the national organization was focusing the majority of its resources, attention, and energies on the most troubled chapters, which were in an endless cycle of pain, while neglecting the chapters with the greatest promise and potential. This was a model that was doomed to continue its downward spiral.

Suzanne and the board lobbied throughout the nation at the chapter level, made the case, and, painstakingly, won the support they needed. They built teams from across the country that included chapter CEOs, local board chairs, and national board members to collaborate together for the first time to arrive at workable solutions. This same team of cross-organizational leaders traveled, called, and persuaded the chapters on the needed change in governance. This was a new beginning of collaborative leadership that was established for the longer term. Once the entire organization was moving forward in agreement on the new structure and direction, the board engaged a national CEO who shared the vision and had the experience and talents to work with the board, the national staff, and the chapters to make the vision a reality.

Suzanne and her colleagues on the board had the insight to recognize the fundamental structural flaws in the organizational model; the professionalism, humility, and sense to engage experts to conduct a proper analysis; the political acumen to build support throughout the national and chapter leadership to lead the change (and identify the right people for this undertaking); the passion and genuine commitment to persuade others organization-wide to the greater organizational potential and the necessary structural changes, and the perseverance to lead the change process. This is leadership.

Not only did Suzanne exercise true leadership, so did the individuals on the national board, at the local and regional levels, and throughout Make A Wish Foundation. They all played a part in creating a new vision and restructuring the model to achieve success. There were many heroes. This was a leadership development experience for all of them.

As a corporate CEO, Suzanne Sutter was already a leader. Nonetheless, Suzanne attests to the tremendous personal and professional growth she experienced as a result of having chaired Make A Wish Foundation. Before accepting the role of national chair, she met with each of her senior executives at Things Remembered to gain their support; the result was that each of them accepted greater strategic responsibility within the company. Suzanne explains, "I learned that I had to make choices in terms of time and focus. With my executives' commitment and support, I was able to steer the strategic course of the business even when the workload intensified with MAW. Through this time we transformed our business through new ownership and hit our financial targets." Not only did Suzanne learn to delegate and stay focused on strategy, she also developed a far greater appreciation of the importance of celebrating life. "The experience taught me to honor and appreciate those who are dealing with the realities of ill health. It also reinforced that life is about celebrating every moment."

> *The nonprofit boardroom is the perfect environment for leadership development.*

Suzanne and her company have been honored in the field of cause-related marketing for Things Remembered's creative campaigns for MAW. The company raised and donated $1 million to MAW in 2005, a 47 percent increase over the prior year, with the full participation of company associates at stores throughout the nation. One of the lessons of this story is that the personal and professional growth, including leadership development, flourished among people throughout Things Remembered as well as Make A Wish Foundation.

Benefits for Businesses

Leadership development conducted at this scale can become a powerful new dimension of corporate social responsibility. A company can truly distinguish itself among customers, the media, and civic decision makers when its executives are leading the social sector regionally, nationally, and globally, through volunteer governance. A company that supports quality board participation will earn its reputation and image for leadership and integrity, while having a relevant impact in strengthening communities worldwide. At the same time, its executives and professionals will develop the skills to lead the company.

According to PricewaterhouseCoopers' Barometer, a 2003 survey of top executives in large, multinational businesses spanning technology, financial services, and consumer and industrial products and services, community involvement is rated very low among senior executives' priorities in managing for sustainability. ("Governance and corporate ethics," by comparison, rate very high, as they should.) Perhaps community involvement would rise on the scale if it moved beyond basic philanthropy and volunteerism to the sphere of leadership development. Businesses invest vast sums in graduate educations for their executives; nonprofit board involvement is the boot camp for leadership development, and it yields benefits to the community at the same time.

Advantages for Individuals

Those who engage on boards by design, commit themselves to meaningful participation, and function as catalysts for change usually find the experience highly rewarding. They distinguish themselves among their peers and develop as true leaders. The commitment may consume some personal energy, but people are fueled by passion, creativity, and camaraderie. Furthermore, those who are entrepreneurial will often find nonprofit organizations open to envisioning innovative ways in which they can best serve the needs of the community and generate resources to make that possible.

The nonprofit board career path needs to involve thoughtful choices and advancement. Prospective leaders should regard their board experience as their "volunteer career path," with an upward trajectory that parallels their job career path.

Opportunities for Nonprofits

Nonprofits desperately need people who are committed to the organizations' missions and who bring businesses skills to the boardroom, along with access to vital resources. Most of us have heard nonprofits cry out for board members who can write checks. Indeed, it is important for board members to be personally generous and for their employers to support their participation financially.

Nonetheless, the greatest financial value that board members bring is the ability to diagnose the revenue model and see what changes can be made to expand opportunities for the organization to serve its mission. For example, most health and human services organizations depend heavily on government funding; hence, advocacy and public education are engines to increase potential support for vital services provided by the agency. This is an area where board members can add serious value. On the other hand, arts organizations often depend more on charitable support, so outreach for additional corporate and foundation grants and private philanthropy will be more important.

In all cases, for all nonprofits, the board needs to understand what more can be done when the board is generous in giving and raising money and increasing resources. Additionally, once the board understands the key strategic and financial challenges and opportunities, and the revenue model in particular, the board is in the best position to identify and recruit the kinds of candidates it needs in order to advance its own work.

Maximizing the Potential

Business, nonprofit, and civic leaders who see the unrealized potential of nonprofit boards can do much to improve governance while developing new leadership by investing in effective board matching programs as well as board training, coaching, and consulting services. Ideally, high-quality board matching programs should be based in regional nonprofit organizations that have local expertise and relationships and a community interest. At the same time, however, high standards of performance need to be established and implemented.

Nonprofit board experience has too often been a high-risk, low-reward experience. When board matches are random, the results are random too. When the matching process is lackluster, the results are lackluster too. Historically, board matching has been almost completely random. When the training is uninspiring, new board members begin their service accordingly. If instead boards and candidates are matched thoughtfully and purposefully, and candidates are prepared as agents of opportunity and positive advancement, then every party benefits to the fullest.

Board candidates and boards must be matched based on a high-quality process involving serious needs assessments of each nonprofit, candidate interviews and "career counseling," and thoughtful introductions based on mutual interests between boards and candidates. It is not simply a matter of matching the person to the mission. It is also necessary to match the candidate to the nonprofit's environment and culture. New board members become agents of change; the introduction of any new person alters a group dynamic, and if matches are done well, the change will be positive.

Nonprofits also need to be supported with robust board and organizational training, coaching, and consulting in order to advance boards, strategies, and strategic alliances.

Envision the Future

There are three levels of nonprofits. The top tier draws the best, brightest, wealthiest, and most influential board members in the world. These are organizations like Carnegie Hall and its peers. They comprise the top few percent of nonprofit organizations. At the bottom, financially, are the grassroots organizations, which do heroic work serving the neediest in our communities with few paid staff members (if any). Their boards and their finances are usually in daily crisis and a continuous cycle of pain; they never know how to get a leg up.

The real opportunity is in the vast middle. This grand mass of nonprofits, with budgets from $300,000 to $10 million (and many ranging up to $100 million in the case of health and human services), provide myriad services with which we are familiar: offering day care to children of all backgrounds, running our smaller museums as well as programs at zoos, botanical gardens, and neighborhood centers, educating children with disabilities, sheltering the poor, operating soup kitchens, and performing concerts and plays in local parks and churches. These organizations are most in need of board candidates who are ready to rise to the duty of imagination: to envision the greater potential, to lead the way by imagining the potential, inventing grander revenue models, generating greater resources, and granting more wishes.

Volunteer board service is the great opportunity for leadership development. In the interests of corporate as well as global sustainability, it is time for businesses to invest in leadership development through nonprofit board participation. By elevating the performance of the nonprofit sector through high-impact service, businesses and their talented executives can help lead the way for communities, and the world, to be a better place. ∎

The Leadership Difference:
Executive Intelligence

BY JUSTIN MENKES

Some businesspeople lead and manage so effortlessly and effectively that it seems like magic. But can you pull aside the curtain that conceals their artistry to discover the specific skills that make them so exceptional? Actually you can. What distinguishes them is a remarkable facility for the critical thinking skills necessary for managerial work, what I call Executive Intelligence. It is these skills that we must seek to develop in ourselves and in the people we hire.

Unfortunately, these skills are quite rare, and the vast majority of executives act without thinking. Does that sound harsh? Consider what one of the most published authors on managerial decision making, McGill University professor Henry Mintzberg, wrote in a 1973 book titled *The Nature of Managerial Work*. He brought together the findings of hundreds of studies involving senior and middle managers, hospital administrators, and chief executives. His in-depth analysis revealed that people rarely employ rational or linear approaches to problem solving, and they almost never make decisions by trying first to understand what the actual problem is that they are addressing. Instead, they take immediate action, groping their way toward a solution through trial and error. Mintzburg's research revealed that acting without thinking is how the vast majority of managers do their jobs.

Have things changed since Mintzberg's book came out? Gillette's CEO, Jim Kilts, laughed when I asked if he could think of a recent example that highlights the tendency of executives to act without thinking.

"Probably one every day. . . . One I can think of right away involved the reorganization of the sales force at Nabisco. A consulting firm had come in and did a big study. They told Nabisco they could save $60 million if they could eliminate the dual role of the sales rep, and divide the existing sales force into two separate jobs. One would be purely responsible for selling, and the other would be responsible for servicing the customer. . . .

"So that's what Nabisco did. They figured, 'Well, we need to save some money and using this model would save $60 million, so let's do it.'

"But those responsible for the decision never questioned the assumption that separating sales and service roles was a good idea. It turned out that once they separated the two roles, people did *neither* well. Those who were selling couldn't get customers to listen to them because the service part was so screwed up. But the salespeople couldn't explain why the service part was screwed up because they no longer had responsibility for it. It was no longer their problem.

"The customers only wanted to see one face; they wanted one person in charge of their store. So when Nabisco divided executional responsibility they never critically examined the assumptions under the new model. It was contrary to what the customer wanted, and it was contrary to what Nabisco could practically manage. It was ready . . . fire . . . then aim. That one was really costly."

Acting Without Thinking

Critical thought plays little role, if any, in many executives' activities. The problem is compounded by the widely accepted fallacy that as long as managers are busy they are doing their jobs well, even though they often commit their time and resources to actions that are unlikely to be fruitful and may even be counterproductive.

Justin Menkes heads the Executive Intelligence Group. His book, "Executive Intelligence: What All Great Leaders Have," is based on eight years of research, including interviews with outstanding leaders such as Jack Welch, Kevin Rollins, and Andrea Jung. As a partner with Spencer Stuart, Menkes consults with businesses throughout the world to help them identify, hire, and promote exceptional leaders and managers. His clients include Hewlett-Packard, J. Crew, BskyB, and DuPont, among others.

Andrea Jung, CEO of Avon, explained why leaders behave this way:

"The pace of business is furious. The textbook leadership process and the real process are not the same. Problems come quickly, not in slow motion. That is the source of why there is so much 'ready, fire, then aim.' But you have to maintain decision-making rigor, because when you lose that, and you're just winging it, that's when problems generally happen. The loss of this discipline is what is responsible for so many people jumping without thinking."

No matter the costs of such action-first behavior, in most cases it is encouraged and even rewarded. When Karen Jehn and Keith Weigelt of the Wharton School studied decision-making styles, they demonstrated that managers, particularly in Western cultures, have a high regard for anyone who orders immediate action. Unfortunately, few skills are applied to ensure that these actions are the best way to reach the right goal.

In this environment, individuals who pause to question actions or goals risk being considered "hesitant to take charge." Leadership norms that scream "Don't think—act!" have supported these behaviors. Denigrating thoughtful action helps perpetuate a system that neither recognizes the necessity of critical thinking skills nor nurtures their development.

Although a review of relevant information— the use of probing questions, and on-the-spot, careful deliberation—all lack the immediate "launch into action" mode that we delude ourselves is necessary in today's fast-paced world, these activities are ultimately the quickest approach to achieving optimal results.

Dell's leaders have proven themselves able to make thoughtful, deliberate moves that yield positive results far faster than their competitors. While Dell's leaders are acutely aware of the crucial need for speed in today's competitive environment, their understanding of how to actually deliver such speed is unique. Kevin Rollins, Dell's CEO, describes how Dell goes about balancing speed with sound reasoning:

"We believe a strategy does not have to be completely baked before launch. However, we do not believe in hunches. So with a foundation of analytics, and good data, and good assessment, we will launch. And we will fine-tune and correct along the way. Though we want to get moving fast, the difference between our method and the gut launch is that there is a lot of data analyzed. We don't want to protract the data assessment and analytic phase, we want to get moving. So we do a lot of experiments, learn, refine, and then go. But we only do this if we feel the idea has potential after our initial analysis.

"For instance, we made the decision to enter printing and imaging, networking, and consumer electronics—because the data showed that our model would work. We said this looks pretty good, and it has all the characteristics of a good one. So let's launch it, and we'll refine it as we go. But we don't do things on hunches or gut instincts at Dell. Everything we try comes from a sound analytic base."

Rollins is referring to Dell's use of critical thinking at every stage of their strategy development and execution cycle. Their extraordinary pace of implementation proves that critical analysis does not hinder quick decision making. Yet with today's emphasis on speed, sound analysis has been overlooked. Critical inquiry is all too often seen as an impediment, when in reality it must be acknowledged as a catalyst of effective action. Any sound analysis should always include recognition of the time constraints involved, the depths of analysis required to make a good decision, and the potential costs of lost opportunity. Those factors create a natural guide as to how complete the analysis should be, and they allow the circumstances to determine the scope of the deliberations.

The delusion that critical thought is a hindrance to fast results has never been more dangerous to organizational success. Action-oriented managers often argue they do not have time to get something right the first time, yet somehow they find the time to redo it three or four times. In an accelerated business environment you have one shot, not three, to get a decision right. And just as a good golf swing takes no more time than a bad one, the good swing gets you to the hole much more quickly. Asking the right questions when facing a complex decision is no more time-consuming than asking the wrong ones. In fact, it saves time. Yet few executives can perform such critical inquiries.

Sound analysis recognizes time constraints and the potential costs of lost opportunity.

Critical Thinking for Leaders

Recognizing that there is a type of critical thinking that is directly relevant to business has made possible the discovery of Executive Intelligence, which refers to one's capacity for critical thinking in all aspects of executive work. Because of their superior critical thinking, star executives arrive at the right answers more often than their peers. But what is the magic behind their success? Is there some secret formula? Theorists and business professors have tried for years to answer that question, touting their work as "the" guide to sound decision making. But the truth is that there is no magic formula. This is exactly why so many MBAs trained in the best decision-making paradigms fail in the real world. The secret behind the stars' success lies in their ability to create a solution tailored to suit each situation at hand.

Quinn Spitzer and Ron Evans of KepnerTregoe, an international management consulting firm, also noted this pattern in their research regarding the world's most successful leaders. How, they asked in their national best-seller *Heads You Win,* could Sam Walton build Wal-Mart without an MBA; Jack Welch make GE into the most admired company in the world without ever going to business school; and David Packard make HP an industry leader without "business process reengineering"? None of those men had the formal training that is meant to ensure business success. So could there be something more fundamental to performance than the theories taught in business schools and management books? Spitzer and Evans identified that there was, in fact, a basic determinant of executive success that was totally distinct from the knowledge gained in a business education.

They discovered that the great executives throughout recent history were not just people of action but also people capable of thought—*critical thought.* With the precision of hindsight, Spitzer and Evans concluded that the critical thinking that leaders like Jack Welch, Sam Walton, and David Packard brought to bear in their businesses was fundamentally more effective than that of their colleagues and competitors. Their superior thought processes enabled them to better assess complex economic environments and identify quick responses to central business issues. When problems arose, they could accurately identify the causes and quickly take corrective action. They made good decisions, balancing the benefits and risks associated with their choices. And they implemented their chosen course of action effectively by circumventing problems and seizing opportunities.

Jack Welch expressed similar views when I interviewed him:

"I don't care if an executive went to a top business school. That doesn't matter to me. It's more about a way of thinking, something I call a 'healthy skepticism.' There's no question that great leaders are constantly looking around corners, anticipating and 'smelling out' issues. For instance, when a deal came to me I always approached it with the premise that the price was too high, or that it didn't fit with our business. I'd then probe to try to see and prove why it fit, what was good about it, and how it would change us for the better. It's about smelling out what's really going on. Asking the right questions and anticipating problems is a big aspect of leadership. What we are talking about is the granular stuff of business. A leader must have that."

What Welch refers to as the "granular stuff of business" is, in fact, critical thinking. The skills he describes—probing, proving, asking the right questions, anticipating problems—are the specific cognitive skills that make up critical thinking.

Careful deliberation is the quickest route to optimal results.

So what is critical thinking, and how does it determine an executive's effectiveness? Traditionally, critical thinking has been associated with exercises involving simple logic games. A typical question might be: All mallards are ducks, and all ducks fly, therefore all mallards can *what* (a: quack, b: swim, c: eat, d: fly)? But how is this abstract exercise relevant to business decision making? We must take a closer look at critical thinking and its relevance to leadership.

In its simplest form, critical thinking in business involves skillfully working out the best answer you can come up with by identifying and using all information that has value for that purpose and resisting irrelevant or unreliable considerations, however tempting they may be. This is not easy, but then again, there are no shortcuts to finding the optimal way to handle a particular situation. Critical thinking is the best guide we have for discovering the "right answers."

The key is to stop looking for paradigms to solve business problems and recognize the inescapably organic nature of on-the-job decision making. It is the aptitude for critical thinking in business that determines the quality of the approach and the results, not training in the latest, best-practice problem-solving techniques.

In reality, business critical thinking is a form of intelligence—an organic, adaptive, ever-evolving set of cognitive skills applied in the business arena. It is the skill base necessary for effective leadership.

So what are these skills? Three subjects are essential for managerial work. Executives must be able to accomplish tasks, understand other people in order to work with and through them, and accurately judge themselves and adapt their behavior accordingly. Each of the three categories involves some predictable aptitudes:

When *accomplishing tasks,* executives who do this well
- Question underlying assumptions effectively.
- Anticipate unintended consequences of various tactics.
- Define a problem appropriately.
- Differentiate essential objectives from less relevant concerns.
  - Anticipate likely obstacles to achieving objectives and identify sensible means to circumvent them.

Regarding *understanding people,* executives who handle interpersonal situations well
- Recognize underlying agendas.
- Gauge how these agendas may conflict with one another.
- Anticipate the probable effects and likely unintended consequences of a chosen course of action.
- Understand how those involved are likely to react and weigh this information appropriately in their responses.

In *judging and adapting their own behavior,* executives who are smart about themselves
- Recognize their own mistakes and minimize the costs of these missteps.
- Seek out and encourage constructive criticism and use it to make appropriate adjustments to their plans of action.

> ■
>
> *Asking the right questions is no more time-consuming than asking the wrong ones.*
>
> ■

- See their mistakes quickly when they blunder and change course to correct the problem.
- Recognize when criticism is baseless and know when to stand their ground.

The Broad Role of Executive Intelligence

Executive Intelligence is crucial to decision making in any position of leadership, not just at the CEO level. It dominates leadership performance across industries in the public, private, and government sectors. But, as with any theory, it is necessary to look to real-life examples to fully comprehend how theory translates into actual behavior.

After the tragic events of 9/11 in New York City, Washington, D.C., and Pennsylvania, the American Red Cross set up the Liberty Fund to collect money for the victims and their families. Massive amounts of donations flowed in, totaling more than $564 million. But then a shocking secret was leaked—more than half of the money collected would not be going to the intended victims. It was being set aside for Red Cross administrative costs and future needs.

The Red Cross president at the time, Dr. Bernadine Healy, exacerbated the situation when she testified before Congress and vigorously defended the organization's actions. "The Liberty Fund is a war fund. It has evolved into a war fund," she said. "We must have blood readiness. We must have the ability to help our troops if we go into a ground war. We must have the ability to help the victims of tomorrow." Fund contributors and government regulators reacted with outrage. A highly public Congressional investigation was launched.

In allocating the money for purposes other than what its donors intended, the Red Cross leadership showed a troubling inability to anticipate the *likely emotional reactions* of donors and government regulators. Making matters worse, when Dr. Healy was confronted with the reality that she and her organization had terribly misjudged public opinion, she stubbornly rejected the criticism as unfounded. In Executive Intelligence terms, she showed an inability to *recognize when serious flaws in her actions required swift acknowledgment of the mistake and a dramatic change in direction.* As a result of the Red Cross's missteps and Healy's failure to acknowledge and correct them, thousands of contributors called to find out where their money had gone and to demand refunds.

Effective executive action always calls for the ability to turn a critical eye on your own thinking and behavior. Whether in a strategy planning meeting, a one-on-one exchange, or any other business format, leaders must be able to test the limits of their own ideas against those of others. This is not to suggest that skilled executives are robots that do not feel emotions like defensiveness, but rather that they can recognize their own mistakes without being blinded by other reactions.

The Red Cross example illustrates how leadership decisions can be analyzed in terms of the cognitive skills that are at the core of Executive Intelligence. By doing this, the underlying causes of a manager's success or failure can be more readily understood.

Executive Intelligence is the essential internal compass that ultimately determines how skillful an individual's actions will be. This does not mean that star executives do not listen to their instincts or to outside expertise; it's just that they use their Executive Intelligence in deciding when to listen and how much attention to pay. While it is useful to learn from the successes and mistakes of others, Executive Intelligence is not just another template or paradigm that instructs people in the steps needed to make a decision. It is more of an explanation of how exceptional minds think and how brilliant decision making occurs. ∎

The Activist and the CEO

Two new books take on corporate America from very different directions. The first, not surprisingly, is by a political activist who accuses many of America's best-known companies of poor corporate citizenship. The second is by a successful CEO who *also* charges that top companies often fail to meet their corporate responsibilities. But although the activist and the CEO make similar accusations, their suggested solutions are diametrically opposed.

In *The Great American Jobs Scam: Corporate Tax Dodging and the Myth of Job Creation*, author Greg LeRoy argues that Wal-Mart, Dell, Fidelity Investments, Boeing, IBM, and a host of other blue-chip companies are all part of a $50 billion-a-year scam that plays states and cities against each other to win tax subsidies in the guise of providing jobs. It's an all-too-familiar story, LeRoy says: a large company promises to move into a community and create well-paying jobs, or threatens to leave and lay off workers. In each case, the author says, the price demanded is huge tax breaks and other subsidies from state and local governments. Furthermore, he argues, in case after case, these promises—of good jobs and higher tax revenues in exchange for massive taxpayer subsidies—prove false or exaggerated. Instead, LeRoy argues, companies are using the promise of jobs to fuel bidding wars among both states and localities. The end result: a massive drop in corporate taxes and a burden shift onto working families and small businesses.

According to LeRoy, the average state has more than thirty subsidy programs that range from property tax abatement, corporate income tax credits, and infrastructure aid to straight-out cash grants. He argues that companies are routinely getting subsidies of more than $100,000 per job to do what they would have done anyway. In some cases, companies even downsize or outsource after getting subsidies—or relocate existing jobs and call them "new." The other promised benefit—increased tax revenues—often proves false or exaggerated as well.

The book offers what the author calls "simple, common sense reforms" including "strict accountability measures" and grassroots organizing to make the job-subsidy system more transparent and effective. Not surprisingly for an activist, the solutions to the problems he portrays are largely political.

The CEO also lays some heavy charges against corporate America. The CEO in question is Leo Hindery of InterMedia Partners, a private equity firm, and former CEO

CEOs can't claim that social issues aren't their concern.

of GlobalCenter, AT&T Broadband, and the YES network. Hindery's book is *It Takes a CEO: It's Time to Lead with Integrity.* Hindery doesn't directly address the charges Greg LeRoy makes, but he does forcefully argue that companies and their CEOs can't look the other way and claim that social issues aren't their concern. The title, *It Takes a CEO,* doesn't mean "that CEOs are all-knowing or all wise," he says. "The point is that CEOs have a special role to play in our society. Because of the way our society is hardwired, there are certain things that only a CEO can tackle." He goes on to say that if CEOs don't take their responsibilities seriously, "What's at risk is the entire way of life that we've come to treasure in America."

Hindery isn't talking about the charlatans and crooks, the Ken Lays and Dennis Kozlowskis. "There's a far bigger bunch who don't have . . . skeletons in their closets but unfortunately have nothing to point to on the positive side of the ledger either. When you say to these guys that it takes a CEO, they tend to blink uncomprehendingly and ask, 'Well, to do what, exactly?'"

Hindery points to many problems we face, the "overconcentration of power in this country," the race to the bottom—a "competitive downward spiral in our economic, cultural, and political lives," excessive unemployment, poor access to health care, outsourcing, and other concerns. Companies, and their CEOs, ignore these growing problems at their peril. "America's best days can be ahead, but not if we continue on the course we are on," he writes. "We need to change course. We need to steer toward a new shore. That shore is in sight. But it will take a CEO (multiplied by the hundreds, and the thousands) to help us get there."

Only CEOs have the clout to draw the line and say no, Hindery says. And his book details a number of CEOs who are drawing lines against outsourcing, the race to the

bottom, poor access to health care, and other concerns. One example he cites is Costco's CEO Jim Sinegal, who has drawn the line against the race to the bottom in terms of employee pay and benefits—and who still competes successfully against Wal-Mart.

Comparing the CEO's and the activist's solutions seems to suggest that if leaders do not step up to take responsibility, the answer may be more political action and regulation.

PUBLIC LEADERSHIP

Lifelong Lessons from Brian O'Connell

·

The leadership of many executives is visible only inside the organizations they lead. Those outside, if they know about such a leader at all, usually see the leader as a spokesman for the organization, and do not witness the leadership skills and abilities deployed within it. These leaders might be called private leaders. But there are also public leaders as well, leaders who pursue public causes and the common good—work that by its nature must be visible and public. And we don't mean those in gov-

ernment—whose "leadership" may consist only of following the polls. We are talking about leaders who build coalitions in either the private, public, or social sectors—or even across these sectors.

One such leader is Brian O'Connell, who with John W. Gardner founded Independent Sector, the national umbrella organization for philanthropy and voluntary action, and served as its president and CEO for 15 years. O'Connell has had a lifetime of organizing for public causes, beginning at the local level and extending to national and international crusades. He began his career serving in various leadership positions at the American Heart Association, finishing as director of its California affiliate. In 1966 he was appointed national director of the Mental Health Association, a position he held until 1978. He then became president of the National Council of Philanthropy and executive director of the Coalition of National Voluntary Organizations, which merged in 1980 to form Independent Sector. In the 1990s, he helped establish CIVICUS: World Alliance for Citizen Participation.

Throughout O'Connell's career he has bridged the worlds of action and writing, publishing 14 books and many articles. His first book, *Effective Leadership in Voluntary Or-*

ganizations, was published in 1975. His latest, *Fifty Years in Public Causes,* has just recently been released.

Fifty Years in Public Causes traces a lifetime of organizing in pursuit of important causes involving health, mental health, participatory democracy, and more.

"People who get involved with public causes open themselves to frustration and disappointment," he writes, "but—through it all and after it all—those moments of making change happen for the better can be among our lasting joys. There is something wonderfully rewarding in being part of an effort that makes a difference. And there's something rewarding in being among other people when they're at their best too."

Currently a professor of citizenship and public service at Tufts University, O'Connell emphasizes the important responsibilities of citizenship throughout *Fifty Years in Public Causes.* He writes, "I'd like to think that careers like mine have helped widen the public's understanding of who and what is included in public service, extending not only to diverse careers but also to America's vast network of volunteers and to the concept of citizens and the primary office holders of government." He believes that everyone should be prepared to live a life of active citizenship and service to society. And he worries that, despite Americans' willingness to be active volunteers in their communities, there is evidence that "most Americans, including a

Live a life of active citizenship and service to society.

majority of high school and college students, are not inclined to have much to do with government." He concludes the book with recommendations "for those going forward" on rectifying this trend to achieve high levels of citizen participation in government and society. Certainly a fitting objective for a man who has spent a lifetime as a public leader. ∎

For More Info...

Additional readings and resources on the topics referred to in this issue.

■

Ten Rules for Leaders

Charles F. Knight
Performance Without Compromise: How Emerson Consistently Achieves Winning Results (Harvard Business School Press, 2005; 304 pages; $29.95)

Moral Intelligence for Successful Leadership

Doug Lennick and Fred Kiel
Moral Intelligence: Enhancing Business Performance and Leadership Success (Wharton School Publishing/Prentice Hall, 2005; 304 pages; $25.95)

Jim Collins
Good to Great: Why Some Companies Make the Leap . . . and Others Don't (HarperCollins, 2001; 320 pages; $27.50)

Good to Great and the Social Sectors: Why Business Thinking Is Not the Answer (Jim Collins, 2005; 42 pages; $11.95)

www.moralcompass.com

■

Reversing America's Corporate Brain Drain

David Heenan
Flight Capital: The Alarming Exodus of America's Best and Brightest (Davies-Black, 2005; 232 pages; $24.95)

www.flight-capital.com

■

Inside-Outside Leadership for Exponential Growth

David Thomson
Blueprint to a Billion: 7 Essentials to Achieve Exponential Growth (Wiley, 2006; 288 pages; $27.95)

www.blueprinttoabillion.com

■

Renewing and Sustaining Leadership

Annie McKee And Richard Boyatzis
Resonant Leadership: Renewing Yourself and Connecting With Others Through Mindfulness, Hope, and Compassion (Harvard Business School Press, 2005; 240 pages; $25.95)

■

Passing the Torch of Leadership

Hewitt Associates
Top Companies for Leaders (Hewitt Associates, 2005; 20 pages; available online: http://was4.hewitt.com/ hewitt/resource/rptspubs/ subrptspubs/top_companies _2005.htm; access date Dec. 8, 2005)

Robert P. Gandossy, Ellissa Tucker, and Nidhi Verma
Workforce Wake-Up Call: Your Workforce Is Changing, Are You? (Wiley, 2006; 272 pages; $34.95)

James C. Collins and Jerry I. Porras
Built to Last (HarperBusiness, 1999; 368 pages; $27.50)

■

Developing Visionary Leaders

Alice Korngold
Leveraging Good Will: Strengthening Nonprofits by Engaging Businesses (Jossey-Bass, 2005; 240 pages; $34.00)

www.alicekorngold.com.

■

The Leadership Difference: Executive Intelligence

Justin Menkes
Executive Intelligence: What All Great Leaders Have (HarperCollins, 2005; 336 pages; $27.95)

Henry Mintzberg
The Nature of Managerial Work (HarperCollins, 1973; out of print)

Karen Jehn and Keith Weigelt
"Reflective versus Expedient Decision Making; Views from East and West," in *Wharton on Making Decisions*, edited by Stephen J. Hoch and Howard C. Kunreuther, with Robert E. Gunther (Wiley, 2001; 339 pages; $29.95)

Quinn Spitzer and Ron Evans
Heads, You Win! How the Best Companies Think (Fireside, 1999; 304 pages; $18.95)

■

The Activist and the CEO

Leo Hindery
It Takes a CEO: It's Time to Lead with Integrity (Free Press; 208 pages; $24.00)

Greg LeRoy
The Great American Jobs Scam: Corporate Tax Dodging and the Myth of Job Creation (Berrett-Koehler, 2005; 290 pages; $24.95)

■

Lifelong Lessons from Brian O'Connell

Brian O'Connell
Fifty Years in Public Causes: Stories from a Road Less Traveled (Tufts University Press; 228 pages; 24.95)